Helping English Language Learners Succeed

2nd Edition

Author
Carmen Zuñiga Dunlap, Ph.D.

Foreword
Sonja Bloetner, M.A.

SHELL EDUCATION

Image Credits

p.87, 189, Photos.com; p.190 Dreamstime; p.254, Janelle Bell-Martin; All other images Shutterstock

Shell Education

5301 Oceanus Drive
Huntington Beach, CA 92649-1030
http://www.shelleducation.com

ISBN 978-1-4258-1188-4

© 2015 Shell Educational Publishing, Inc.

Helping English Language Learners Succeed

2nd Edition

Table of Contents

Foreword

I have worked in the field of education for over 20 years, as an English for Speakers of Other Languages (ESOL) teacher, curriculum writer, and central office administrator to support the linguistic and academic needs of English language learners at all grade levels. During this time, I have witnessed many shifts in the expectations and accountability for English language learners brought about by federal legislation, such as the *No Child Left Behind Act* of 2001. These shifts have led to the increased monitoring of academic achievement and attainment of English language proficiency for these students. This, in turn, has created the necessity for all educators to expand their instructional tool boxes to better support the academic success of English language learners across all classrooms.

As we move further into the 21st century, it is critical that new resources be developed to support the professional learning needs of educators so that they can adjust their instructional practices to better meet the academic needs of English language learners. *Helping English Language Learners Succeed, 2nd Edition* is one such resource that outlines practical steps that educators can take to support these students across the curriculum.

Carmen Zuñiga Dunlap does a phenomenal job helping readers understand many of the key factors that impact the success of English learners in both content and English language development classrooms. In this resource the author highlights the fundamentals of language learning and effective English language development in the four skill areas of listening, speaking, reading, and writing. She also emphasizes the importance of explicitly teaching academic vocabulary during instruction.

Dr. Zuñiga Dunlap provides very practical strategies to help teachers plan with the end in mind as they design lessons and units of study to effectively meet the linguistic and academic needs of English language learners. She also does an excellent job of engaging readers as they explore their own knowledge and beliefs, beginning each chapter with an anticipatory quiz.

Next, she focuses on specific actions that educators can take to build the academic and language skills of English language learners who encounter new learning in the oral and written contexts of the classroom. Finally, she guides readers to reflect on the steps that they will take to apply these ideas to the practices evident in their classrooms.

She highlights research about how motivation impacts language learning, driven by student qualities such as positive task orientation and the need for achievement. She also emphasizes that oral language skills are the building blocks of conceptual development in the content classroom, leading to academic success. In addition, she clearly articulates that explicit instruction on features of the English language, such as syntax, grammar, and vocabulary in the context of academic discourse can support the language development of English language learners.

Carmen Zuñiga Dunlap does a fine job outlining the characteristics of various language measures, as well as practical strategies, that can be used to monitor students' progress toward greater language proficiency in English. As well, she challenges readers' beliefs and encourages them to propel English learners toward greater proficiency in writing, highlighting how the understanding of form and fluency and the application of the writing process impact students' ability to communicate effectively in English.

This resource is an excellent addition to any educator's library because it highlights effective ways for teachers to implement simple instructional strategies to enhance their impact on the student learning and improve academic outcomes over time.

Sonja Bloetner, M.A.
Author of *Strategies for Formative Assessment*
with English Language Learners
ESOL Supervisor of Montgomery County Public Schools
Rockville, Maryland

Acknowledgments

While writing is solitary work, I find that it can only occur with support from others.

Many thanks go to Maribel Rendón of Shell Education for her gentle ways, constant availability, and willingness to help me work through dilemmas and deadlines; and to Nicole LeClerc for her suggestions, fine-tooth-comb editing, and perceptive "catches."

I would like to thank my three daughters, Sabrina, Madeline, and Gabriela, for their continuous encouragement and enthusiastic support; and my grandsons, Julius and Fabian, for sharing with me their experiences with their own literacy development.

For my husband, Burnie—without whose initial encouragement, daily support, patience, and clarity of thinking as my sounding board this undertaking would not have been possible—my love and my gratitude for providing me the time and peace of mind to be able to disappear into a quiet thinking and writing space.

Introduction

Four framing questions inform this book:

- What are best practices for teaching English language learners?
- What are the theoretical foundations of these best practices?
- What do these best practices look like in the classroom?
- How can teachers use these best practices to help their English language learners succeed?

Experienced teachers with increasing numbers of English language learners, novice teachers who seek additional professional development, teachers who want to incorporate the Common Core State Standards for English Language Arts (CCSS for ELA) to more intentionally support English learners, English language development / English as a second language curriculum coordinators seeking ways to assist classroom teachers, and ELD/ESL teachers outside the United States looking to further support students in overseas settings will find professional support in the chapters ahead. This book details classroom practices and approaches that support listening and speaking, vocabulary development, reading comprehension development, and writing development. These practices, approaches, and strategies are anchored in established key constructs, theoretical frameworks, and current research findings. Many are examples taken from both novice and veteran classroom teacher practices, and the author's teaching experiences. Woven throughout the chapters are teaching suggestions that help English language learners develop the competencies required by the Common Core State Standards.

How This Book Is Organized

The chapter topics follow a logical flow. Chapters 1 and 2 provide essential background information. Chapter 3 outlines classroom-based assessment strategies for English language learners. Chapters 4 through 7 focus on specific aspects of the language arts. Chapter 8 provides a lesson and unit design model. You may read the chapters in sequence, or you may read according to your particular needs and interests. The chapters address the following topics:

- Chapter 1, "Teaching English Language Learners: 21st Century Contexts," describes the many current influences on English learners.

- Chapter 2, "Understanding Language," addresses language and language learning fundamentals.

- Chapter 3, "Assessing Language," examines classroom-based language assessments.

- Chapter 4, "Developing Listening and Speaking Abilities," presents listening and speaking strategies.

- Chapter 5, "Building Vocabulary," looks at vocabulary development.

- Chapter 6, "Helping English Learners Who Are Reading to Learn," discusses reading for comprehension.

- Chapter 7, "Teaching Writing," addresses writing development for English language learners.

- Chapter 8, "Thinking through and Organizing for Instruction," offers guidance in planning curriculum for mixed groups of English learners and fluent English speakers. It is based on the idea of backward planning and demonstrates how a teacher might prepare for teaching a thematic unit.

At the beginning of each chapter is an Anticipatory Quiz to activate thinking about the chapter's content. At the end of each chapter is a set of Apply, Reflect, and Extend questions that encourage thinking about and applying the chapter's content to your own teaching circumstances.

Substantial additions and modifications have been made to this edition of *Helping English Language Learners Succeed*. These include new chapters on developing vocabulary, teaching reading comprehension, developing listening and speaking abilities, and thinking through, and organizing for, instruction. Modifications and additions have been made to the chapters on language and language learning, assessment, and teaching writing. Teaching considerations guided by the Common Core are incorporated throughout.

Terminology Used in This Book

Educational terms abound when describing English language learners, their English language progress, types of educational settings, and suitable lesson design. The following list serves to clarify terms used in this book:

- ELD refers to *English language development*. ESL refers to *English as a second language*. They appear as ELD/ESL in this book because they both refer to the complete scope and sequence of curricular programs that help students develop specific English language skills, or they refer to this type of focused English language instruction.

- There is no agreement across states and agencies about what to call the stages of English language development. Because ELD/ESL occurs along a continuum, it is possible to set demarcation lines and labels at any point. Some states use three categories to describe the stages (e.g., in California: *emerging*, *expanding*, and *bridging*). Other states use four categories (e.g., in Texas: *beginning*, *intermediate*, *advanced*, and *high advanced*). World-Class Instructional Design and Assessment (WIDA) and the state of New York use five stages of development (*entering*, *emerging*, *developing*, *expanding*, and *bridging*). For the sake of neutrality and simplicity, the categories used in this book are *beginning*, *intermediate*, and *advanced*.

Chapter 1

Teaching English Language Learners: 21st Century Contexts

Anticipatory Quiz

Are the following statements true or false?

_____ **1.** Teaching English learners simply requires implementing good teaching practices.

_____ **2.** Specific language learning assessment is needed to assist English learners in acquiring academic English.

_____ **3.** Motivation to learn a second language is largely internally driven.

_____ **4.** Oral language development is a critical and often overlooked aspect of learning a second language.

_____ **5.** English learners should focus on learning academic vocabulary rather than learning academic language.

_____ **6.** The learning expectations for English learners make for a challenging fit with the expectations set by the Common Core State Standards.

This chapter looks at some 21st century influences on English learners, within the contexts of the rise of English as a global language, research findings and their influence on how English is taught and learned, and the ways in which the Common Core State Standards are shaping curriculum and instruction for English learners in the United States.

International Context: The Rise of English as a World Language

As of the new millennium, the year 2000, an estimated 1 billion people, or roughly 14 percent of the world's population, were learning English as a second language. By 2025, data convincingly suggest that this figure will reach as high as 2 billion (Graddol 2006). A quick round-the-world glimpse drawn from a variety of contexts helps us understand these statistics:

- The language of international transportation communication is English. Air traffic control personnel and airline pilots, ship captains, and port authority personnel communicate in English.

- English, rather than French or German, is now the preferred and most commonly used language among European Union members.

- Students pursuing advanced degrees in non-native English-speaking countries use textbooks written in English due to both the proliferation of technical knowledge and the sheer number of textbooks published in English.

- In the United States, the number of English learners enrolled in public schools increased 67 percent between the 1994–95 school year and the 2008–09 school year, with the current English learner population at 5.2 million (U.S. Department of Education, Office of English Language Acquisition 2010).

- In the United Kingdom, the British Office of Education reports that between 1995 and 2012, the English learner population increased 100 percent, from 500,000 to 1,000,000 students, representing one in six at the primary school level and one in eight at the secondary level (National Association for Language Development in the Curriculum 2012).

Driven by business, technology, international transportation communication, the entertainment industry, and unprecedented world migration, English has become a world language. It is by and large the common denominator for communication around the world, requiring vast numbers of teachers. Teachers of English learners, then, are members of a large and vital worldwide community who seek to improve and expand knowledge, expertise, and teaching approaches to help students meet their learning needs and goals.

Research Context: Knowledge About Teaching and Learning English

We continually learn and apply new knowledge and positive research outcomes to educational practice. The following sections outline six aspects of teaching and learning English in the context of information drawn from research findings.

English Learners Need More Than Just "Good Teaching"

While effective teaching strategies are generally beneficial for all students, data now show that high-quality reading instruction by itself is not sufficient to help English learners improve text comprehension (Goldenberg 2008). In addition, Diane August and Timothy Shanahan state that adjustments in approaches to teaching reading and writing are needed in order to provide "maximum benefit with language-minority students" (2006, 3).

English Learners Need Precise Assessment

We now know that English learners often need more careful assessment—in addition to standardized English language assessments—to determine gaps in their language learning. Identifying and addressing gaps in academic language is especially important (Dutro and Levy 2012). This information gives teachers a close-up view of an English learner's needs, and is the first step in helping a student achieve academic success.

English Learners Need Support and Motivation

Second language learning research suggests that learner motivation can be both self-regulated as well as teacher enhanced (Oroujlou and Vahedi 2011; Ardasheva, Tong, and Tretter 2012). Teachers can support their English learners by:

- helping students develop and set their own short-term language learning goals;

- creating a positive classroom atmosphere that is predictable, structured, and emotionally safe;

- providing students choices in materials and learning activities;

- promoting a sense of competence by creating situations in which the students will experience success; and

- using assessment approaches that highlight ways that students take note of their own successes.

Qualities or characteristics that effective language learners demonstrate are as follows:

- **Positive task orientation:** Willingness to take on challenging tasks with a sense of competence and confidence in one's ability

- **Need for achievement:** A need to take on new tasks and succeed

- **Goal orientation:** Awareness of learning goals or specific learning tasks and direct attention to achieving them

- **Perseverance:** Consistently investing effort in the learning task or goal

- **Tolerance of ambiguity:** Not becoming unduly frustrated about temporary confusion or lack of understanding (Daskalovska, Gudeva, and Ivanovska 2012)

Students and teachers, in partnership, can establish positive learning outcomes.

English Learners Need Oral Language Development

Oral language skills are the building blocks of conceptual development and the tools we use to express what we know. These skills provide the ability to listen with understanding and to continually build upon words and concepts. Oral language is the means through which children under the age of about twelve most readily take in information (Biemiller 2003; Hirsch and Hansel 2013). According to Claude Goldenberg (2008), "ELLs need intensive oral English language development, especially vocabulary and academic English instruction" (42). Good oral language development sets students on the pathway to academic success.

English Learners Need Direct ELD/ESL Instruction

Past theory maintained that mere exposure to English provides sufficient experience to learn English as a second language, just as young children learn to speak the language that surrounds them (Krashen and Terrell 1983). However, "the natural approach," as it is called, has been replaced with support for direct language instruction for English learners. There is now evidence that English learners make more language progress with specific and direct instruction during a dedicated period of time when they receive "explicit instruction on features of English such as syntax, grammar, vocabulary, pronunciation, and norms of social usage" (Goldenberg 2008, 42) coupled with multiple opportunities to use English for real communication purposes.

English Learners Need Academic Language Development

James Cummins (1981) proposed that English learners face two distinct types of language learning: basic everyday spoken communication used for social interaction (*basic interpersonal communication skills*, or BICS) and the considerably more demanding language used in academic settings (*cognitive and academic language proficiency*, or CALP). Recent research has focused on the topic of academic language, defined as "the specialized language, both oral and written, of academic settings that facilitates communication and thinking about disciplinary content" (Nagy and Townsend 2012, 92). Developing academic language is the cornerstone of English learners' school success.

Academic Context:
The Common Core State Standards

English learners must develop the ability to think critically and creatively, and to express these abilities in English. The Common Core State Standards are inextricably linked with language and language development, and so they fit well with promoting language development and learning for English learners. The Common Core (2010) expects students to interact with peers and teachers in more intentional ways about academic content, requiring the development of speaking and listening skills. They demand that students perform close reading and analysis of text, which necessitates developing good comprehension and critical-reading abilities. They require students to source, assess, and synthesize information, and to express cogent and compelling arguments, all of which require excellent research, writing, and speaking skills.

"Big picture" points that can help teachers embed the Common Core in instruction for English learners are as follows:

- Develop familiarity with the relevant ELD/ESL standards (state or governing body) to understand what English learners should know and be able to do.

- Compile a bank of effective strategies for English learners to draw from and incorporate into instruction.

- Use backward planning. What are English learners expected to know and be able to do? What activities and strategies can help students attain these expectations? What assessments indicate they have achieved the expectations?

- Arrange opportunities for fluent English speakers and English learners to learn together.

Looking through a closer lens, teachers of English learners should:

- select important concepts and vocabulary that students need to know;

- select strategies to teach the important concepts and vocabulary, and to help students build their own understanding;

- develop and implement both content objectives and academic language objectives;

- teach students the relevant text structures of the material to be read or discussed;

- build conversational structures so that English learners can more readily participate in discussion; and

- help students learn ways to look for common ideas across texts and to synthesize the material.

The chapters that follow provide information on all of the preceding points and offer practical ways to help English language learners succeed.

Summary

This chapter examined some major influences that impact how we teach English as a second language today. The fact that English has taken center stage as a world language means that the number of people learning English as a second language is on the rise. Reviewing current research on language and literacy acquisition and development helps educators implement teaching approaches that facilitate second language learning. In addition, the Common Core State Standards significantly shape curriculum and instruction in the United States.

Apply, Reflect, and Extend

1. What types of oral language development are provided for English learners in your setting? What types of regularly scheduled and specifically focused ELD/ESL instruction are provided?

2. What approaches are effective in teaching academic language? Why might these be effective or ineffective with English learners?

3. Describe both your professional development experiences and your particular needs with regard to teaching English learners.

Chapter 2

Understanding Language

Anticipatory Quiz

Are the following statements true or false?

_____ **1.** Linguists have developed broadly accepted stages of second language development.

_____ **2.** English learners are able to draw on their knowledge of language systems in their primary language to help them develop English.

_____ **3.** Correct prosody when reading aloud can indicate that a student is reading with comprehension.

_____ **4.** Students should be discouraged from speaking a language other than English in the classroom.

_____ **5.** There is a difference between grammar and syntax.

An effective teacher of English learners understands the basic elements of language and language development. Why does understanding how language works matter? First, language is the fundamental "tool" of a teacher's daily work. Whether using language to describe a mathematical process or to discuss character development in a story, whether listening to students or reading their written work, language provides the basis for communication. You want to understand how the tool you constantly use works. Second, understanding the various elements and systems of language better equips you to guide your students through the complexities of learning a second language. You are better positioned to help them through the process.

This chapter discusses the basic aspects of this fundamental teacher's "tool," beginning with the eight elements of language.

Eight Elements of Language

Language is so much a part of our environment that we may not give it much thought. It is difficult to imagine life without it. Through language, we express our thoughts and emotions. It is the fundamental form of human communication.

How can language be defined? At bare minimum, language is a series of arbitrary sounds strung together that permit a group of people to communicate. However, it is much more than this. It is a universal human phenomenon that is the foundation of communication. It is systematic and rule governed; it permits transmission of ideas; it is intertwined with culture; it includes regional, social, and economic class variations; and it is affected by where and with whom we use it. Let's take a closer look.

Language does all of the following:

- develops naturally
- develops in stages
- is structured
- is intertwined with culture
- is linked to cognition
- includes variety
- is learned in social and academic contexts
- is influenced by purpose, context, and audience

Language Develops Naturally

Humans acquire their first language largely by hearing it and by interacting with speakers in their environment. The same cannot be said about learning to play the piano, learning to ride a bike, learning to write, or taking on any other complex activity. It is a unique and intricate learning process. Three fundamental theoretical approaches offer insights into how humans learn language: nativist, social interactionist, and cognitive.

Noam Chomsky's (1968) work provided the initial theoretical foundation for the nativist view of language learning. This view holds that humans are born with a biological predisposition to language learning that is supported by a mechanism called the *language acquisition device* (LAD). Proponents of this view believe that language learning is innate and uniquely human. They suggest that the LAD is "hardwired" with a set of rules called *universal grammar*. Exposure even to small amounts of language permits a child to learn rules that pertain to that particular language in a relatively short period of time. Once the child learns the rules, he or she can then create or generate unique sentences based on the internalized rules of that language.

Social interactionists believe that the key element of language learning resides in meaningful social interactions within a supportive environment. Lev Vygotsky (1978) is the individual closely associated with this view of language learning, although his work also reflects his firm belief that language is strongly linked to cognition. He proposed that language has its roots in social interaction and is used as a tool to communicate. Initially talk is only out loud but becomes internal, self-directing, self-regulating speech. Vygotsky proposed that learning is incremental. The term *zone of proximal development* describes Vygotsky's view that the lower limit of a zone is what a child can do independently, while the upper limit is the potential skill that the child is capable of with guidance provided through social interaction.

We associate the work of Jean Piaget (1969; 1990) and Jerome Bruner (1974) with cognitive theories of language learning. This view supports the idea that language learning is directly linked to stages of cognitive development. Piaget's work suggests that language occurs naturally as children move through stages of cognitive development. At the preoperational stage, for example, children talk about the concepts they learn, such as counting and classifying, and they use past, present, and future tenses to talk about events in time. For Bruner, cognition and language are inextricably linked. Bruner believed that the way we make sense of information is by classifying and categorizing it, with great importance attached to developing the language that expresses it. He believed that academic language needs to be taught so that students can demonstrate that they can process and understand information and use it for problem solving.

Each theoretical approach contains intuitively appealing aspects. A stance that blends elements of all of them might read as follows: Babies are born with an innate language learning ability that differs from other types of abilities. This ability enables them to begin to discriminate meaningful sounds in their language environment soon after birth. They begin to put together and learn to say meaningful sounds, and to grasp the structures of language soon thereafter. Additionally, language and cognition develop in conjunction; growth in one area promotes growth in the other. Language is used as an indispensable tool to express thoughts and ideas. The more exposure to thinking and ideas through language that children have, the better developed their language skills become. The language-learning process is a human and naturally occurring phenomenon that develops in strikingly similar ways across cultures, languages, and geographical locations.

Classroom Application

Teachers can create learning environments for English learners that take advantage of all aspects of the theoretical stances described in this section. For example, children under the age of about eight respond very well to an environment that capitalizes on their innate language learning abilities. They can make remarkably quick advances when immersed in a rich language-learning environment that is accompanied by direct language instruction.

All students benefit from social interaction that offers both language modeling and opportunities for specific peer assistance in academic tasks. While we know that the full range of second language learning cannot occur exclusively through exposure and social interaction, they are powerful ways to support second language development.

Older students, particularly those who have had the advantage of primary language literacy instruction, can use aspects of a cognitive approach to learning in general and to second language learning in particular. They should be given opportunities to apply their general knowledge, literacy skills, and primary language knowledge to learning English.

Language Develops in Stages

First language development begins at birth. Evidence suggests that newborns have already begun to "sort" distinct sounds into those that carry meaning, turning their heads when they hear sounds that carry meaning and ignoring sounds that do not carry meaning in the language in which they are immersed. Within weeks of life, a baby's vocalization consists of crying, gurgling, cooing, and other minimal random sounds. During this time, the infant is taking in enormous amounts of auditory information. This early period provides the foundation for later language development. Within a few short months, babies begin babbling. Linguists suggest that these sounds may provide a baby with practice for throat, mouth, and tongue movements in preparation for speaking. These precursors to language turn into a baby's first recognizable words around the age of twelve months. Figure 2.1 presents broadly accepted stages of first language development from infancy to forty-eight months.

Figure 2.1 Stages of First Language Development from Infancy to 48 Months

Stage	Age Range	Description
Stage I	0–6 months	Active listening; beginning to attend to meaningful phonemes in the environment
Stage II	6–10 months	Gurgling, cooing, babbling; playing with patterns of speech sounds and rhythms; repetition of phonemes
Stage III	10–18 months	One-word stage; individual words, usually two repeated syllables (*ba-ba*, *ma-ma*) that are discernable and attached to people and objects in the environment
Stage IV	18–24 months	Two-word utterances called "telegraphic speech" because meaning is reduced to its most basic communication (as telegrams used to be written); point at which grammar begins to emerge in that two-word utterances have relationships to each other ("Daddy sock," "Doggie out")
Stage V	24–30 months	Multiword stage; longer phrases; vocabulary increases by about 3 words per week, and up to 10 words per week after the child knows about 40 words; vocabulary at 24 months is normally between 200 and 300 words
Stage VI	30–48 months	Vocabulary acquisition rate can increase in the third year and beyond at an average of about eight words a day during preschool and elementary school years

Second language development also occurs in stages; however, there are no generally accepted terms or recognized stages. Because language learning is a continuum, descriptors can be developed for any point along the continuum without great impact. Figure 2.2 presents a selection of descriptors taken from four different sets of ELD/ESL standards. The labels of developmental stages bear little similarity to each other, besides indicating a progression of language development.

Figure 2.2 Examples of Labels of Developmental Stages

Agency and Release Date	Stages of Development				
California Department of Education October 2012	Emerging		Expanding		Bridging
Kansas State Department of Education March 2011	Beginning	High beginning	Intermediate	High intermediate	Advanced
Texas Education Agency 2012	Beginning	Intermediate		Advanced	High advanced
World-Class Instructional Design and Assessment (WIDA) 2012	Entering	Emerging	Developing	Expanding	Bridging

While it is possible to create labels for developmental stages along the language continuum, four important elements should be addressed:

- Each label should be supported with a description of that stage, including descriptions for listening, speaking, reading, and writing.

- The stages should align with the assessment system that is used so that clear benchmarks can be established to help the teacher guide instruction and learning expectations.

- Teachers need a clear understanding of the instructional consequences of the developmental stage.

- Assessments should be used regularly to ensure improvement over time.

No matter the stage of English language development, the preceding fundamental elements should be included. Moreover, the following should also be included:

- meaningful opportunities for using all four language domains of listening, speaking, reading, and writing

- language modeling in all four domains

- specific and direct ELD/ESL instruction

- ongoing assessment and student feedback loops both for English language development and for content instruction as relevant to the teaching/learning setting

It is helpful to keep in mind the developmental path of a child's primary language when it comes to predicting how long it will take an English learner to acquire English proficiency. Consider an infant's active listening for several months, comprehensible utterances that begin at twelve months, and literacy skills that the child is able to achieve with some proficiency at the sixth or seventh grade, which are then continually refined with additional years of education. Now think of an English learner who must start anew in another language. English learners pass through the preproduction stage to the intermediate period within two to three years. An additional three or four years are required to achieve adequate literacy skills, given a consistent and high-quality education. What a child works at for many years in the primary language will take time to fully develop in a second language—language learning takes time. English learners need time, patience, and consistently high-quality instruction to succeed.

Teachers may see students passing through various stages of English language development. Also evident may be each student's own pace of developing English. Taking into account the student's level of English both guides instruction and is a strong indicator of the work that the student is capable of understanding and producing.

Language Is Structured

Imagine listening to the speech of someone who has *a way with words*. We don't usually think about the underlying structure that makes up this pleasing "whole." Yet we could. We might, for example, begin to notice the descriptive verbs the speaker selects, or a particular cadence of speech, or ways the speaker artfully puts phrases together. Each of these is representative of one of the systems of language.

The systems of language discussed in this section are linguistically universal—they exist in all languages. So English learners bring a vast amount of inherent knowledge of language structure in their first language to the process of learning English. They rely on familiar ways that their primary language works to help them learn and navigate English.

Students' knowledge and reliance on their first language can be very helpful. For example, when a student understands that there are ways of expressing concepts such as past and future tenses, relationships between and among people and objects, time, and so on, he or she seeks specific ways to express these concepts in English. An effective teacher will find ways to capitalize on a student's knowledge of his or her primary language, as well as encouraging the student to use his or her own knowledge of how language works to promote teaching and learning English.

Phonology

Phonology is the study of sounds. The smallest unit of sound is called a *phoneme*. An example of a phoneme is *n* or /n/ as a linguist writes it. Of the entire range of humanly possible sounds, only a subset is included in a particular language. At just weeks old, babies begin to experiment with making the entire range of possible sounds, or phonemes. They attend to the sounds around them that seem to carry meaning, ignoring those that do not. So from infancy, babies begin building a bank of meaningful sounds in the language they will learn to speak.

There are rules that govern how a language puts sounds together to make words. In English, a rule allows us to place /n/ and /d/ in the middle or at the end of a word—as in *indeed* or *stand*—but not at the beginning of a word. In Swahili, a phonological rule permits /n/ and /d/ at the beginning of a word—as in *ndiyo*, meaning "yes" or "it is so." Any single sound or combination of sounds that does not exist in one language but does exist in another will create difficulty for a second language learner to pronounce.

Classroom Application

The most difficult sounds to hear are those that do not carry meaning in an individual's primary language—those that the individual has not attended to from birth. A person's inability to hear a certain sound means that the person cannot distinguish that sound as carrying meaning or significance, which is the whole point of phonemic awareness: being able to hear and say certain sounds and being able to manipulate them in speech. We place children at a great disadvantage when we ask them to listen for particular sounds and hear the difference between them, when these differences do not exist in their primary language. So, for example, asking Spanish-speaking children to distinguish short vowel sounds in English, which do not exist in their primary language, is an exceedingly difficult task for them. This linguistic reality in the Spanish language bumps up against an English language reality: in English, starting phonemic awareness and early reading with short vowel sounds makes sense, given the usefulness of short vowel sound rimes, or word families. However, teachers should be aware of just how difficult it is for a child to hear and begin to read sounds that the child never knew existed and has never used.

Morphology

Morphology is the study of meaningful units of sound. A *morpheme* is the smallest unit of meaning. There are two types of morphemes: free and bound. A *free morpheme* carries its own meaning, like *hat* or *desk*. *Bound morphemes* consist of prefixes, suffixes, and inflected endings such as *-s* or *'s*, or *-ed* or *-ing*, and must be combined with other words. Inflected morphemes are grammatical markers. Young children and English learners begin to use and manipulate inflected morphemes in useful and sometimes curious ways as they become proficient. Consider the morpheme *-y*, meaning roughly "full of," as in *rusty* or *dusty*. A three-year-old was overheard referring to someone as *singy*, meaning "someone who is full of song or who likes to sing." Morphological use indicates that a finer-grained understanding of language is in process.

Classroom Application

Prefixes, suffixes, root words, and inflected endings are useful and productive morphemes for students to learn. The CCSS Reading: Foundational Skills Standards and Language/Vocabulary Acquisition and Anchor Standards specifically include the study of affixes, and root words as a focus, beginning in the first grade. About 60 percent of academic English words consist of a morpheme that always carries the same meaning. Being able to break apart words and unlock meaning is a very important strategy for English learners to learn and use.

Prosody

Prosody refers to the stress, pitch, intonation, and rhythm of words and phrases. Research reports "conversational turn-taking" that occurs between caregivers and babies who cannot yet form words, based on the prosody of the exchange of phrases. This indicates that there are standard prosodic features that carry more meaning beyond just the words and phrases themselves. It also indicates that prosody carries emotional and feeling-tone information. Moreover, it shows that individual sounds and prosodic patterns are the first acquired aspects of language. Using appropriate prosody in spoken language indicates the individual is a fluent speaker of that language.

> "[Prosody] reflects the reader's understanding of the structure of sentences, punctuation, and to a large extent, the author's purpose."
>
> —Zarrillo (2011, 66)

Figure 2.3 shows an example of altering prosody, a simple sentence like "You're driving to the store" can carry entirely different meanings depending on stress, pitch, and intonation.

Figure 2.3 Sample Prosody Statements

Phrase Stress, Pitch, or Intonation	Meaning
You're driving to the store. (falling intonation)	And you promised me we'd go on a picnic.
You're driving to the store?	What? You **never** go to the store!
You're **driving** to the store?	What? But don't you always just walk there?
You're driving to **the store**?	But you never go shopping!
You're-dri-ving-to-the-store!	Yes! You're going to go get a pound of hamburger, and I don't want to hear another word about it!

Classroom Application

Using appropriate prosody in oral reading is important because it is a strong indicator that a student is reading with comprehension.

Conversely, flat, monotone, and word-by-word or syllable-by-syllable reading without the use of appropriate prosody indicates that the student lacks automatic decoding skills, is laboring through words, and is not capturing the meaning of the text. The first step to ensuring that a student can read with appropriate prosody is to establish that the student can automatically decode words, based on a firm grasp of phonics, and can read high-frequency words. Repeated reading, shared reading, and sharing marked text with appropriate prosodic markings can help a student improve in this area.

Syntax

Syntax is the system of rules that govern how words are arranged to form meaningful phrases and sentences. Syntax accounts for the word order, or linear order, of a sentence or a phrase, and the meaningful groupings of words called *constituents*. Syntactic rules allow for play on words and sentences with double meanings, or they can guide literary license to writing or speaking. Syntactic rules also explain how paraphrased and ambiguous sentences are related, as well as how a sentence can be infinitely expanded. An example of paraphrasing is "Whenever she goes on vacation, it rains" and "Why does it seem to rain whenever she goes on vacation?" The underlying syntactic structure of "It rains whenever she goes on vacation" would support both sentences. Paraphrasing occurs by moving constituents around, which is governed by syntactic rules.

Syntactic rules also account for and describe meanings in ambiguous sentences. Chomsky's (1965) well-known example, "Visiting relatives can be annoying," can mean either that having to visit relatives can be annoying or that having relatives who come to visit can be annoying. Underlying syntactic rules clarify this ambiguity of meaning.

Finally, syntactic rules describe how a sentence can be expanded into an increasingly longer sentence, or can be *recursive*, to use the linguistic term. An example of recursion is "Terry threw on his jacket and scarf" and "Terry, throwing on his tan jacket and orange scarf, ran helter-skelter out the door." Understanding syntactic rules, or the underlying structure of sentences, enables us to understand paraphrasing, ambiguity, and recursiveness, and allows us to manipulate sentence constituents.

In contrast, *grammar* can be thought of as a set of rules that govern what constitutes correctness or the proper surface structure of language. Whereas grammar helps us produce correct sentences, syntax allows for language creativity and license. Thus, an individual who understands and can manipulate the syntax of a language has a deeper understanding of that language than someone who can only create grammatical sentences.

Semantics

Semantics is the study of the meaning of words, phrases, and sentences. Describing meaning is a much more fluid proposition than describing rules that govern other aspects of language in a systematic way because meaning is influenced by use in context and by cultural and individual aspects. However, there are two categories of semantics that linguists have written about. The first is *structural semantics*, which is the study of how meaning is found in small units, and how the composition of an interrelated system of units and structures work together to create meaning. More useful here is an understanding of the second category, *lexical semantics*, which focuses on meaning that is carried in the use of words. Figure 2.4 shows some lexical semantics terminology that influences meaning and provides examples to contextualize them.

Classroom Application

Teachers of English focus on teaching the rules of grammar. English learners who begin to use plays on words or sentences with double meanings in their speaking and writing are developing a deeper understanding and sophisticated sense of the subtle workings of English. More advanced English learners working to improve their writing skills may find aspects of syntax helpful—for example, learning to play with constituent placement in sentences and experimenting with how constituent placement can convey weight and meaning differently.

Lexical semantics can be a useful way to approach vocabulary building for advanced English learners and long-term English learners.

Figure 2.4 Lexical Semantics Terminology

Lexical Semantic Term	Definition	Examples
Incompatibility or antonymy	Words used in a sentence that carry "oppositeness" of meaning.	• the attention span of a gnat • as steady as the wind
Connotation	Words that suggest or imply an underlying meaning. Examples are *universe* and *wind. Universe*, for example, connotes vastness. *Wind* connotes fast or changeable.	She has a whole universe of information in her head.
Markedness	An unmarked term can be • the default term • the basic word with no inflections or affixes • the masculine or singular form of a word	The unmarked term appears first: • actor/actress • lion/lioness • honest/dishonest • shaven/unshaven • marked/unmarked • happy/unhappy

Other lexical terms are more familiar and commonly used. These include antonyms, synonyms, similes, and metaphors.

Pragmatics

Pragmatics considers how language carries social meaning and is used for real-time ongoing communication. Linguists have constructed some categories and principles that describe aspects of pragmatics. For example, the language philosopher Paul Grice (1975) suggested four maxims involved in social interaction:

- **Maxim of quantity:** We shouldn't say too much or too little.
- **Maxim of quality:** We should be truthful and give honest information.
- **Maxim of relation:** We should make relevant contributions to conversation.
- **Maxim of manner:** We should be clear, to the point, and orderly in communicating our thoughts.

Another language philosopher, John Austin (1976), building on Grice's work, described language that we use to get other people to do things for us with our words, referring to this type of language use as *speech acts*. Let's say, for example, a guest in someone's home says, "Gee, it's cold in here." The host may respond, "Let me get you a sweater" or "I'll turn up the heat." The guest has engaged in requesting or convincing. Speech acts describe how we invite, command, pardon, apologize, excuse, and perform a host of other acts. Austin also examined what he called *felicity conditions*, meaning that a sentence can be taken seriously only under a suitable circumstance. An example is "I'm giving you an *A* on this work," which can be taken seriously only if spoken by an authorized person in the appropriate circumstance.

The ways in which we adhere to Grice's maxims in conversation and how we do things with words are culturally embedded. How we invite, decline, greet, and take leave are directly linked to culture. For example, in Japan, it is expected that someone will turn down an invitation by simply saying, "I am not able to come." In the United States, either a form of apology or an explanation, or both, are socially polite and expected.

Language Is Intertwined with Culture

Knowing a language does not necessarily mean that you can navigate through the culture of that language. For example, a common practice in the United States is for children to have sleepovers or slumber parties. It is a common and accepted way for children to "hang out" at a friend's house and have fun into the evening and sometimes beyond. For people of other cultures, allowing their children to sleep in the home of another family, or to sleep anywhere besides at home with their own family, may be an unknown and uncomfortable practice. So not only may the phrase "slumber party" need an explanation, but it may also require becoming familiar with a common concept that is embedded in the culture. Other examples that may need contextual cultural explanations can include the language and practices commonly associated with celebrations and holidays.

Classroom Application

Instruction for English learners should include attention to the use of pragmatics, or how native speakers use English in social contexts. Scenarios and role-playing can be helpful when teaching students how to respond in culturally appropriate ways in English.

It is necessary to not only teach English as a second language, but also help students navigate cultural differences as they become acclimated to new linguistic meanings and cultural traditions or events.

Language Is Linked to Cognition

One theoretical stance of language learning asserts that cognitive development supports language development. Some believe the reverse is true—that language development drives learning and provides humans the ability to organize their thinking. Certainly, there is an undeniable link between the two. Let's look at two examples that illustrate how cognition affects language and, conversely, how language affects cognition.

First, consider a young child who makes the conceptual discovery of "in" and links it to the word. The child begins to use the word over and over again—"in the box," "in the shoe," "in the bed," "in the doggie," and so on. Children delight in making these discoveries, as evidenced by the constant use they make of their exciting new finds.

Next, let's look at an example illustrating how language can influence understanding. A three-year-old became intrigued with the word *area*. She used the word constantly, as in "the silverware area" (the drawers where the silverware is kept), "the desk area" (in reference to her little chair and table with her crayons, paper, and books), "the table area" (the dining table), and so on. Through hearing the word used by others, she began to refine her understanding of it until she came to use the word correctly.

Classroom Application

Learning concepts and vocabulary are inextricably linked. Vocabulary development alone is one of the most challenging aspects of learning another language. Learning concepts in a second language is even more difficult. It involves understanding and learning the vocabulary, and having the language tools at hand in order to be able to talk, read, and write about them. English learners who lack a firm primary language from which to grow or in which to anchor the new concepts are especially challenged. These students in particular require a language-rich and concept-rich environment in which to develop both linguistically and cognitively. Above all else, teachers of English learners must embed learning and vocabulary in understandable contexts.

Language Includes Variety

We can think of language variety in two different ways. First, variety can refer to the scope of sounds and sound systems that are humanly possible. Clicks, nasals, throaty guttural sounds, and tonal variations of a single sound are some examples. A second way we can think about language variety is within a single language. Spoken English varies across regions and socioeconomic classes. Every language has these varieties. A regional variety can be referred to as an *accent* and implies a difference in pronunciation. It might also be called a *dialect* that may include grammatical and lexical variations, as well as differences in pronunciation. An example of a grammatical variation that is not standard English is the use of the word *so*, as in "I *so* don't want to go" (*so* is stressed and used as an adverb rather than an adjective). The use of *so* in this instance has become commonly used, but strictly speaking, it is not grammatically correct. The words *bag*, *sack*, and *poke* are examples of regional lexical variations. They mean the same thing; however, they are used preferentially in different regions of the United States. People typically don't think they have an accent or dialect because they are surrounded by others who speak the same way. We consider our own speech the norm.

Classroom Application

Varieties of spoken English have little, if any, influence on English learners. Only if the spoken variety differs greatly in syntactic structure from standard English might it present a challenge to the English learner.

However, in terms of variation of sounds across language, English learners will have difficulty hearing and pronouncing sounds in English that do not exist in their native languages. Young students who are learning to speak English while learning to read in English can be greatly challenged by sounds in English that they do not perceive. It is important to help young English learners develop the ability to hear sounds first before teaching them to read the symbols.

Language Is Learned in Social and Academic Contexts

Social interaction theorists believe that language learning resides in meaningful social interactions within a supportive environment. Humans are social and curious. We want to be included when we're interested in what's happening around us; therefore, an environment that sparks a desire in the learners to be involved and to know what is going on is critical.

Another important element for the learner is a guide who knows how to listen, explain, answer questions, and negotiate meaning in that environment. For young children, caretakers are the guides who interact in meaningful ways. For English learners, the teacher and classroom peers are the guides who construct meaning through comprehensible language input. Of course, the learner is not a passive recipient. Negotiating meaning is a joint venture. Both learner and guide are partners in constructing meaning. A good guide modifies and adjusts language to the level of the learner for maximum understanding as the learner participates in paying attention and attempting to understand.

English learners need particular attention to develop academic language. As opposed to social contexts, the classroom environment is unique in its position to help students in this regard. Academic conversations, vocabulary development, and multiple opportunities to read, write, and hear academic language modeled are all especially important for English learners.

Classroom Application

The teacher's role is to provide a rich context in which students can engage in learning English. With this in mind, it is important to set up the classroom environment such that students have multiple opportunities to talk to each other as they explain, clarify, complete projects, and construct meaning together. Additionally, a teacher can model for fluent English speakers how to be helpful guides for the English learners in the classroom.

Language Is Influenced by Purpose, Context, and Audience

Just as we wear clothes for different occasions, purposes, and messages we want to send, we also alter the ways in which we use language. For example, wearing a suit to a business meeting is appropriate, but it is inappropriate to wear one to the playground while romping with children. Similarly, speaking with a close family member in a casual manner is very different from conversing with someone you meet for the first time in a formal setting.

The terms *register* and *discourse* are important to understand in the context of this eighth element of language. Register refers to how language varies in relation to purpose, context, and audience, so it is correct to say that register influences or, even more appropriately, governs language use. Register controls vocabulary, sentence structure, stress, pitch, and intonation (prosody), and other linguistic features. Discourse refers to speech or text of some length. A discourse can be a verbal exchange or a conversation, or it can refer to a coherent piece of text that is longer than a few sentences. Register also governs discourse.

Classroom Application

Academic English is a register. English learners need to learn to use this register for academic success. Academic language is anchored in subject matter that employs more refined word selection, uses precise words and language, stays on topic with ideas presented in a logical flow, and features different types of carefully constructed underlying grammatical structures than are used in casual, informal language. Academic language is more difficult to understand and produce, and it is more linguistically and cognitively demanding than informally spoken language. Much of the work of a teacher of English learners is to help students learn to use the appropriate register of schooling—academic English.

Factors Affecting Language Use at Home, in the Community, and at School

While the focus on language so far has been on the elements or principles of language, the sections that follow consider home, community, and school environment factors that also influence language development.

Family Influences

A family's influence on a child is undeniably fundamental. Not surprising, then, are the language influences the family brings to bear. These include which language is primarily used in the home; with whom, when, and where the language is used; and the frequency of use. Parents' views on education and parental involvement are additional factors to consider.

English vs. the Native Language at Home

A student may be the first in his or her family to learn English, or the student may have siblings or other family members who bring English into the home environment and who have paved the way in the educational system. Having other English speakers in the home is helpful. The question sometimes arises about how to encourage parents to speak English to their children at home. The response is to encourage use of the family's primary language. If the parents' dominant language is other than English, then they should speak and, if possible, read with their children in that language. The parents should be encouraged to use the dominant language to the fullest extent possible at home. The reason is that solid development in a language is far more preferable than impoverished English language development.

Parents should tell and read stories, recite rhymes, sing songs, and even watch television together and then discuss what they watched—all in the native language. Parents should talk with their children in the clearest and richest way possible and encourage their children to talk with them in the native language. This use of language helps with concept and vocabulary development. It is using language to its fullest that helps children develop thinking and the language that goes along with it. The work of a teacher of English learners is to teach English and content, and that job is much easier when students have a solid grasp of the first language. It is far better to transfer knowledge from one language to another than to have to develop concepts in a second language. Encourage the use of the parents' dominant language at home as much as possible. An added benefit is that the parents and children can stay linguistically connected. Learning English should not mean losing the home language. One of the most unfortunate aspects of losing the home language is that the student may also lose the ability to communicate with his or her family members.

The Family's Views About Education

Culture affects our values and beliefs in ways we may not even consider. Education is one of these areas of impact. Every culture has its unique way of "doing" education. This includes the notion of what good teaching is, what the curriculum should include, and what it means to be a good student and a good teacher. For example, in some countries the teacher is revered for the knowledge he or she has. It would be unacceptable for a teacher to respond to a student's question by saying, "I don't have an answer for that, but let's find out." However, this response is completely acceptable in the United States. In some countries, students are expected to do a great deal of homework and study long hours. When their children are given what some parents perceive as light homework loads in the United States, by comparison, these parents may worry that their children are not being taught well.

Parental Involvement

Should parents be involved guides? Quietly supportive? Firm advocates for the perceived needs of the child? Hands off because they believe expertise resides in the school and it's best to leave instruction to the teachers? In the United States, parents are expected to be involved, and educators seek ways to involve them. It is important to understand that a teacher's expectations may not match the cultural norm for the student's family. It may be necessary to work at helping parents become comfortable with participating in their child's schooling.

As teachers work with parents to help them become familiar with how schooling is done in the United States, homework expectations, the grading system, test scores and their meaning should all be explained. Conversely, it is helpful to find out as much as possible about how schooling is done in the students' native countries. Having this sort of information can guide a teacher's expectations and provide opportunities to compare and contrast schooling approaches for the parents. While the parents may not feel completely satisfied with the teaching methods, they will appreciate efforts to have differences explained to them. Furthermore, the school may find ways to help them grow to accept the way schooling is done in the United States.

Here are dimensions to consider that can give insight into a culture's view of schooling:

1. Is schooling considered competitive or cooperative?

2. Is individual work valued over group work?

3. Does teaching methodology favor student inquiry or lecture and recitation?

4. Is shared work among students considered cheating or the norm?

5. Are boys and girls segregated or integrated?

6. Are educational expectations and attainment gender driven?

7. Is student improvement over time satisfactory, or is the focus on perfection, excellence, and high grades?

8. Are students expected to focus exclusively on academics, or are other interests, such as sports or music, encouraged as part of the curriculum?

9. Do parents and students expect that high-stakes tests are a normal part of schooling, or are high-stakes tests unexpected or not understood?

10. Are parents accustomed to being involved in school and their children's activities?

Community Influences

In neighborhoods and communities with a single and large non-English-speaking population, there may be little opportunity, reason, or motivation to use English outside school. Most or all aspects of daily life can easily occur in a language other than English. Conversely, in a multilingual community, English usually becomes the common language.

In schools and neighborhoods with a large concentration of a single language other than English, teachers need to find ways to promote and expand ways for students to use English. This is important because in such a single-language environment, the teacher can be the sole English language model. Second language learners should have multiple language models and multiple opportunities to use the second language. Using email and videoconferencing are ways to connect native English speakers and English learners. These modes foster real and meaningful communication, provide fluent English language models, create a real purpose for using English as clearly and correctly as possible, and can be used for social purposes and for structured subject-matter exchanges.

School Influences

Schools and school districts with an English learner population should provide support for classroom teachers, such as up-to-date ELD/ESL curriculum materials and opportunities for professional development in this area. The school should have appropriately credentialed teachers to work with English learners. There may be a newcomer class or, in a large district, a newcomer school exclusively for newly arrived non-English-speaking immigrant students, where students learn basic English and receive cultural orientation. A community liaison that takes care of outreach to parents is an additional support. These are all indicators that the school takes success for English learners seriously and is committed to actively supporting their education.

Teacher Influences

A positive teacher/student relationship is the fundamental and necessary building block for learning. Students who trust and respect their teachers are motivated to learn. A welcoming environment also helps students feel a sense of security and belonging.

Demonstrate Respect for the Primary Language and Culture

The teacher's goal is to help students learn English and grade-appropriate subject matter. Respect for the primary language and culture shows students that the teacher sees learning as a mutual endeavor. Teachers can

- learn to pronounce names correctly;
- invite students to share basic phrases in their language (e.g., good morning, goodbye, see you tomorrow) that everyone can learn and enjoy using on a daily basis;
- display maps marking students' countries of origin, label classroom objects in the students' languages, and play music from various world regions; and
- ensure that all the students' languages are included, as an imbalance in the number of students from a particular language background might make it easy to give a single student's language a quick pass-over.

Teachers can also make diversity and learning about diversity part of the curriculum. Make multicultural education the standard—visually, aurally, and within the curriculum. Here are a few suggestions:

- Do daily or weekly "fast facts"—a few quick facts about aspects of a student's culture, language, or country.
- Invite students to share special holidays and events.
- Encourage students to bring items from home that help other students understand aspects of that student's culture.
- Encourage students to write bilingual stories at school or at home with their parents' assistance, and invite them to share these stories at school.

Learning climates that are respectful and inclusive of students' linguistic and cultural backgrounds help them succeed academically. Conversely, years after schooling experiences, students remember when they have been belittled, alienated, made to feel ashamed or shut out, embarrassed about being different, and perhaps frustrated at not being connected to the curriculum. Recently, a university provost of a large institution, in addressing a gathering of honored educators, shared his experiences as a young non-English-speaking immigrant student. To this day, he explained, he will always remember his first teacher's kindness and support in helping him learn English.

Assign a Buddy

A friendly and inviting way to orient a new English learner is to assign the student a buddy who is an outgoing and nurturing English speaker. Establish a "welcome committee" of English-speaking students to select and groom for this assignment. Give them school maps. Have the assigned buddy show the new student around the school: "This is the bathroom," "Here's the lunchroom." Have the buddy show the English learner classroom routines and where the classroom supplies are kept. English learners will be able to establish a friendship, get anchored in the life of the classroom and school, and learn some English along the way.

Embed Language in Routines

Predictable and consistent routines and language patterns linked with written and visible schedules are helpful in teaching common phrases. By using these routine classroom procedures, English learners understand how the day and week flow, as well as learn vocabulary associated with these routines (Peregoy and Boyle 2013).

English Learners' Influence on the Teacher

Up until now, the focus of this chapter has been on language itself and influences on the students that affect their language learning. Still within the scope of understanding language, this final section reverses the focus. That is, what are the students' influences on the teacher? What are the students' language considerations that impact planning? They are

- the number of English learners in the classroom;
- the number of languages represented in the classroom;
- the stage of English language development of each student; and
- the type of primary language support available.

The number of English learners in a classroom affects how many fluent English speakers can provide language modeling. If only the teacher is a fluent English speaker, the demands on the teacher's language input can be high. Conversely, if there is only one English learner, there is a temptation to skip over this student's English learning needs and focus on instruction for the fluent English speakers. For this reason, the notion of "a critical mass" of English learners in one classroom is important. The students should be placed with a teacher who holds the proper professional preparation and disposition to work with English learners.

The number of languages that students speak in a classroom matters. Having two or more speakers of the same language can be an advantage, especially if one is more fluent in English. A definite plus is to allow them to use their native language to help one another understand and negotiate content meaning. After all, the students' goal is to learn, and so much the better if there is another person who can help convey the content in a meaningful way. English learners' content understanding can be enhanced when provided scaffolding opportunities in the primary language. There are three cautions, however.

- First, constant translation should not be permitted. It can take away learning time from the bilingual student.

- Second, the bilingual student may feel burdened. Working with another student should never be an imposed obligation.

- Third, dependence on someone for translation makes a language learner less willing to work at negotiating meaning in English, and therefore less apt to learn English. Constant translation is not bilingual education, nor is it sound educational practice. However, the available primary language resources should be used to support English learners.

The stages of English learners' development affects preparing comprehensible content instruction. If all the students are at the same level of English development—intermediate, for example—then just one level of lesson preparation is needed to meet learning support. If there are beginning, intermediate, and advanced levels of English learners, each level may require somewhat different approaches and strategies.

Education in the primary language—that is, primary language schooling—and literacy level impact a student's ability to learn English.

The more schooling and the higher the literacy level, the more preparation the student brings to English language learning. A strong primary language background is a key element in being able to learn English, because the student is not struggling to accomplish two tasks at the same time: learning English and learning in English. Rather, the student can more readily focus on learning English. The underlying concept of bilingual education rests on developing strong primary language and literacy skills that the student can then apply to another language. The teacher should take full advantage of primary language support, including student-to-student support, as discussed earlier.

Summary

This chapter outlined the stages of language development and the theoretical views that support its development. You learned about the structures of language and that language is inextricably intertwined with cognition and culture. Finally, you considered the ways in which language is affected by purpose, context, audience, and family and community use. Armed with a better understanding of the fundamentals of how language develops and works, in the next chapters you will learn about specific aspects of language development and ways to help students along the path to English language fluency and subject matter understanding.

Apply, Reflect, and Extend

1. Which theory of language development do you find most convincing and why? How can your theoretical stance affect your classroom practice?

2. How might you use lexical semantics to expand your students' academic language?

3. Describe a situation when an English learner had the words right but was culturally off the mark.

4. What types of academic language development are your students provided?

5. Have you encountered a cultural misunderstanding with a student's family? How was this mitigated?

Chapter 3

Assessing Language

Anticipatory Quiz

Are the following statements true or false?

_____   1. Assessing English learners requires no special considerations beyond those used for fluent English speakers.

_____   2. There is value in separately assessing an English learner's listening, speaking, reading, and writing abilities.

_____   3. English learners who receive rich language arts instruction do not need focused ELD/ESL instruction.

_____   4. Assessing a student's primary language abilities is an important first step in establishing appropriate language instruction.

_____   5. Assessing English learners using rubrics is generally not an effective practice.

"Would you please tell me which way I ought to go from here?" asked Alice.

"That depends a good deal on where you want to get to," said the cat.

"I don't much care where," said Alice.

"Then it doesn't matter which way you go," said the cat.

—Lewis Carroll, *Alice in Wonderland*

The Cheshire Cat's exchange with Alice captures the essence of assessment. If there is no end goal in mind, then direction does not matter. Educational goals matter a great deal; therefore, direction matters a great deal. This is why teaching and learning are best guided by educational road maps. Teachers want to assess where their students are at a given point in time, base instructional planning and teaching on this information to help students achieve the established learning goals, and then find out if students have gotten to the desired point.

How is assessing English learners different from assessing fluent English students? Are there particular factors to consider? Is there specific information a teacher should know or consider? The responses to these questions and other matters pertaining to assessing English learners are addressed in this chapter.

Assessment Types and Purposes

English language learners are assessed in a variety of ways and for a variety of purposes. One type is a standardized, norm-referenced assessment administered or managed by the school district. Data from this type of assessment must be made available to federal and state education agencies. This assessment is typically given once a year to all K–12 students who have not yet been classified as fluent English speakers (O'Malley and Valdez Pierce 1996). The results serve to

- screen and identify students who need English language instruction;

- establish appropriate placement for level of instruction;

- monitor student progress;

- reclassify students to move to a different level or exit the English learner program;

- provide information on program evaluation; and

- establish instructional and student accountability.

Another type of assessment is linked to ELD/ESL programs based on a comprehensive scope and sequence of language development skills. Using such ELD/ESL programs and their assessments that check for student progress is a critical component of the English learner's daily curriculum. Initial assessment is required to guide instruction so that specific language needs can be pinpointed (Olsen 2010). For example, initial assessment may indicate that a student needs to learn past perfect or conditional tenses, or practice using transitional words (e.g., *as a result, in spite of, in other words, in comparison*) in academic writing.

Identifying language-learning gaps is particularly important for long-term English learners. These are students enrolled in ELD/ESL programs for six years or more who have "stalled out at the intermediate level" (Dutro and Levy 2012, 341). These students are able to get by adequately with spoken English, yet they have gaps in academic English language abilities. An example of an ELD/ESL program that includes a "gap finder" assessment for long-term English learners is *E.L. Achieve: A Focused Approach to Systematic ELD*, which helps identify students' specific needs and guide them in appropriate learning.

Students who receive daily focused English language instruction at a dedicated time during the school day using an ELD/ESL curriculum make the best progress in learning English. They need opportunities to learn specific grammatical structures and language conventions, to enrich their vocabularies, and to develop literacy skills (Goldenberg 2008). This focused ELD/ESL instruction complements interaction with fluent English speakers, which provides multiple opportunities to hear authentic language being modeled and opportunities to use English for real communication purposes.

While the data sources just discussed are necessary and helpful, teachers should also seek finer-grained diagnostic information based on a student's classroom language use. A teacher's in-class assessments help guide two aspects of an English learner's needs. First, a teacher's own classroom assessments for listening, speaking, reading, and writing can supplement the assessment results discussed in the preceding paragraphs. Classroom-based assessment can provide a clearer answer to the question "How is my student's English language development progressing?"

Second, information from classroom-based assessments helps teachers answer the following questions about content instruction:

- What level of performance on academic tasks can I expect of my English learners?

- What kind of support and modification of instruction do my students need in content instruction?

- To what extent should I assess my students' content learning in ways that do not exclusively rely on language?

Language assessment and content instruction assessment address different concerns, though they are linked, and development in one affects development in the other. Teachers want information on both types of learning, and they should be assessed separately (Goldenberg 2008). This chapter addresses classroom-based language assessments.

Content Objectives and Language Objectives

Teachers should include both content objectives and language objectives when planning instruction (Echevarría, Vogt, and Short 2012). First, doing so will help students become more aware of those aspects of language and encourage their use. Second, being intentionally mindful of and practicing these objectives helps students improve and more naturally incorporate them into spoken and written language. Third, this practice guides students toward meeting the expectation of the Common Core State Standards that they will be able to use standard grammar.

Here is an example of a content objective and a language objective within a lesson:

Content objective:

Students will describe differences between reflected solar energy and absorbed solar energy.

Language objective:

Students will use transitional words when writing about these differences.

Example of what a student might write:

Lighter colors reflect solar energy; darker colors absorb solar energy. Clouds, snow, light-colored buildings, and Earth's gases reflect about 30 percent of the sun's energy. By comparison, Earth's atmosphere and surface absorbs about 70 percent of solar energy.

It is especially helpful for English learners to apply targeted ELD/ESL language instruction to content-area learning. This gives them the opportunity to incorporate practice and use it for authentic academic communication.

Classroom-Based Language Assessments

Returning to the idea of using assessments as road maps to guide teaching and learning, this section describes classroom-based language assessments that a teacher can use for diagnostic information. These assessments may be used two or three times throughout the year to help track a student's language growth and development.

Determining Primary Language Abilities

It is helpful to determine an English language learner's years of primary language schooling, primary oral proficiency, and literacy proficiency.

These three elements are strong indicators of a student's ability to more efficiently acquire English. First, there is evidence that "the number of years of schooling in the primary language is a predictor of English achievement" (Gunderson 2009, 45). Second, there is substantial evidence that "oral proficiency and literacy in the first language can be used to facilitate literacy development in English" (August and Shanahan 2006, 5). Third, in the case of Spanish-speaking students, "Spanish and English oral-language skills contribute to reading [both] within and across languages" (Miller et al. 2006, 30).

All aspects of primary language abilities serve to support second language learning. Chapter 2 discusses the vast amount of linguistic knowledge that a young child quickly develops, as well as the important role that oral language development plays in learning to read. Reading in the primary language means that the individual has developed important language fundamentals: the basic understanding that meaning can be obtained from text, that written language represents sounds that are placed together to create meaning (in the case of alphabetic languages), and that syntactic and semantic relations exist among words and phrases, sentences, and larger pieces of text.

To obtain information about the student's education level, the following possibilities are offered:

- To establish years of primary-language education, the teacher may need to rely on either the student's self-report or information from family members.

- In-school or in-district bilingual personnel may be available to determine oral language and literacy skills.

- If there is access to primary-language material as well as an estimate of the reading level of the material, the student can be asked to read aloud to help determine the student's reading level in the primary language. It is important to keep in mind, however, that "cold reads" are never recommended. The student should be allowed to preview and silently read the material first.

- Another helpful source for establishing primary-language ability is the student's writing samples (Gunning 2013). The student may be asked to bring a passage to school that he or she has written, or the student may be asked to write a passage at school. The student may then be asked to retell what he or she has written. The writing sample alone, however, can serve as a general indicator of the student's writing ability in the primary language.

English Language Assessments

Figure 3.1 indicates the assessments that a teacher can use for English language assessment in his or her classroom. Each assessment type is discussed in more detail following the chart.

Figure 3.1 English Language Assessments

Assessment	Listening	Speaking	Reading	Writing
Oral language interview	✓	✓		
Oral description of a picture		✓		
Student Oral Language Observation Matrix		✓		
Social and Cognitive Listening and Speaking Anecdotal Record (SOLOM)	✓	✓		
Cloze passage			✓	
Maze passage			✓	
Retelling (oral)	✓	✓	✓	
Retelling (written)			✓	✓
Writing to describe a picture				✓

Oral Language Interview

Research is clear about the critical importance of oral English language development.

> "Extensive oral English development must be incorporated into successful literacy instruction … Literacy programs that provide instructional support of oral language development in English aligned with high-quality literacy instruction are the most successful."
>
> —August and Shanahan (2006, 4)

Some of the most critical work of teachers of English language learners is to immerse their students in rich and meaningful oral language experiences with a great deal of modeling and opportunities for authentic communication. Early assessment provides baseline data, directs teaching and learning needs, and with subsequent assessment, demonstrates the learning and progress that the student makes.

Initial oral language assessment should be simple and direct in order to provide a baseline and a general sense of the student's capabilities. The following ten questions begin with those that can be answered briefly and move on to those that more capable students can elaborate on. Using the same questions for early and subsequent assessment and using the same scoring rubric allow for comparison over time.

1. What is your name?

2. Where are you from?

3. How old are you?

4. Can you tell me what day it is?

5. Can you show me a/the [classroom and school objects such as book, pencil, student, teacher, desk, window, door, etc.]?

6. Name as many objects as you can in this room/in this school.

7. What can you tell me about yourself?

8. What is your favorite thing to do?

9. Can you tell me something that you and your friend do together?

10. What can you tell me about your family?

The difference between question 5 and question 6 is that the student is being asked to identify objects (receptive language) and then to name objects (productive language). First, the student is learning school-based English and may not have the English vocabulary to describe cultural or home-based experiences. Second, there may be cultural, social, or even political reasons to avoid personal questions. For example, a student's family may have moved due to political unrest, they may not celebrate events such as birthdays, or they may not celebrate holidays in the same ways as many of their peers, if at all.

The following are possibilities for further assessment.

Assessment Possibilities

1. Ask the student to name colors, days of the week, and ordinal numbers to 10.

2. Ask the student to count to 20, and to count by tens to 100.

Basic verb tense information can be obtained by asking questions requiring the student to use past, future, and conditional tenses, such as the following:

- What did you do yesterday?
- What did you do at lunchtime?
- What will you do tomorrow?
- Where would you like to go?

The student may be prompted to ask questions of the assessor, indicating the ability to formulate grammatical questions as seen in the following examples:

- Ask me what I did yesterday.

- Ask me what I will do next week.

Oral Description of a Picture

A common verbal assessment is to ask a student to describe events and activities in a picture, such as the one seen in Figure 3.2. A larger image of this picture is found in Appendix D. The following types of information can be assessed:

- subject–verb agreement

- present tense verbs

- present progressive (-*ing*)

- singular and plural nouns

- question formation (What does …? What do …?)

Figure 3.2 Oral Assessment Activity

Student Oral Language Observation Matrix (SOLOM)

This rubric is easy to use, provides a quick assessment of an English learner's oral proficiency, and is appropriate for students of any age. Adapted from the Foreign Service Institute Oral Interview by the San Jose (California) Area Bilingual Consortium, it was later revised by the California Department of Education and is now widely used. The rubric is not commercially published and is within public domain use. What makes the SOLOM especially helpful is that it permits the assessor to evaluate a student's English proficiency on five dimensions of language—comprehension, fluency, vocabulary, pronunciation, and grammar—granting a rating for each dimension independent of the others.

Along the side of the matrix are five language domains, and along the top are the numbers 1 (least competent) through 5 (most competent). Within each coordinate in the matrix is a descriptor that corresponds to the level of proficiency in that dimension of language. The teacher listens to the student's responses, marks the cell that best describes the student's abilities for each of the five dimensions of language, and totals the scores. A score of 19 is generally the minimum to be considered language proficient. The results can be tracked over time to indicate progress. This rubric is an ideal way to assess the student's oral language obtained from the oral language interview suggested earlier.

Figure 3.3 Sample SOLOM Rubric

Language Domains	1	2	3	4	5
Comprehension	Cannot be said to understand even simple conversation	Has great difficulty following what is said; can comprehend only social conversation spoken slowly and with frequent repetition	Understands most of what is said at slower-than-normal speed with repetitions	Understands nearly everything at normal speech, although occasional repetition may be necessary	Understands everyday conversation and normal classroom discussions
Fluency	Speech so halting and fragmentary as to make conversation virtually impossible	Usually hesitant; often forced into silence by language limitations	Speech in everyday conversation and classroom discussion frequently disrupted by the student's search for the correct manner of expression	Speech in everyday conversation and classroom discussions generally fluent, with occasional lapses while the student searches for the correct manner of expression	Speech in everyday conversation and classroom discussions fluent and effortless; approximating that of a native speaker
Vocabulary	Vocabulary limitations so extreme as to make conversation virtually impossible	Misuse of words and very limited vocabulary make comprehension quite difficult	Frequently uses the wrong words; conversation somewhat limited because of inadequate vocabulary	Student occasionally uses inappropriate terms and/or must rephrase ideas because of lexical inadequacies	Use of vocabulary and idioms approximate that of a native speaker

Language Domains	1	2	3	4	5
Pronunciation	Pronunciation problems so severe as to make speech virtually unintelligible	Very hard to understand because of pronunciation problems. Must frequently repeat in order to make him/herself understood	Pronunciation problems necessitate concentration on the part of the listener and occasionally lead to misunderstanding	Always intelligible, although the listener is conscious of a definite accent and occasional inappropriate intonation patterns	Pronunciation and intonation approximate that of a native speaker
Grammar	Errors in grammar and word order so severe as to make speech virtually unintelligible	Grammar and word order errors make comprehension difficult; must often rephrase and/or restrict him/herself to basic patterns	Make frequent errors of grammar and word order that occasionally obscure meaning	Occasionally makes grammatical and/or word order errors that do not obscure meaning	Grammar and word order approximate that of a native speaker

(Adapted from California Department of Education)

Social and Cognitive Listening and Speaking Anecdotal Record

This oral language proficiency measure relies on the teacher's observations. English learners are likely to be reserved in the early stages of second language development and then more willing to speak in increasingly larger groups as their ability and ease increase. It is also easier for a student to use English for social purposes than for cognitively based verbal tasks. This assessment, shown in Figure 3.4, helps capture the student's listening and speaking abilities for social and for more intellectually difficult language uses.

Figure 3.4 Social and Cognitive Listening and Speaking Anecdotal Record

Directions: Observe the student for one day or during two to three periods. Then, complete this form by circling the appropriate usage category and writing observations.

Student name: _____ **Date:** _____

	Skills being observed	Comments
Cognitive Domain ↕	**1.** Responds to instructions one-on-one small group whole group	
	2. Gives instructions one-on-one small group whole group	
	3. Talks about/responds to a story one-on-one small group whole group	
	4. Describes real events one-on-one small group whole group	
	5. Describes imaginary events one-on-one small group whole group	
	6. Answers a question (lower level) one-on-one small group whole group	
	7. Asks a question (lower level) one-on-one small group whole group	
	8. Answers a question (higher level) one-on-one small group whole group	
	9. Asks a question (higher level) one-on-one small group whole group	
	← **Social Domain** → (one-on-one ⟶ whole group)	

Printed with permission from Zuñiga Dunlap and Marino Weismann 2006

Figure 3.5 shows a completed form for a student named Marisela. This anecdotal record profiles a student who speaks in one-on-one and small-group settings but is reluctant to do so in a whole-group setting. She uses concrete language, such as answering factual text-based questions, using her textbooks to help her scaffold her responses. She does not yet use English for inferential, evaluative, or imaginative purposes, which are more abstract language uses and therefore more difficult for an English learner. However, she demonstrates the ability to engage in creativity and abstract thinking in a nonverbal task she imaginatively completed.

Figure 3.5 Example Social and Cognitive Listening and Speaking Anecdotal Record

Skills being observed	Comments
1. Responds to instructions (one-on-one) (small group) whole group	Marisela responds well when spoken to individually or when she is doing table work with a small number of students. Social conversation is easier for her than content-specific language. Marisela falls behind when instructions are given to the whole class. She often seems distracted and "tunes out" when the teacher speaks at length. She does not ask questions in whole-group setting.
2. Gives instructions one-on-one small group whole group	Not observed.
3. Talks about/responds to a story one-on-one (small group) whole group	In small groups, Marisela responds to questions about stories that have been read to the students when she is called upon. However, she does not seem to volunteer answers.
4. Describes real events one-on-one (small group) whole group	During two small-group social studies lessons, Marisela offered answers (text-based) when called on, using correct vocabulary and grammatical language.
5. Describes imaginary events one-on-one small group whole group	Marisela has not been observed describing imaginary events, even when other students are doing so.
6. Answers a question (lower level) (one-on-one) (small group) whole group	Marisela responds to friends' questions such as, "What are you doing?"
7. Answers a factual question one-on-one small group (whole group)	During a science lesson, Marisela was able to respond correctly to a few questions. She did not volunteer but answered when called on.
8. Asks a question (higher level) one-on-one small group whole group	Marisela does not appear to ask for additional help or ask a question to better understand something. She is hesitant to ask a question at any level.
9. Answers a question (higher level) one-on-one small group whole group	Although Marisela does not voluntarily answer any questions, she appears to have non-verbal abilities that demonstrate a higher level of thinking. For example, she easily discerns and duplicates block patterns, and she creates her own patterns. She selects the odd item from a series of pictorial events, and creates a logical pictorial series of events on her own. She completed several pictorial analogies (e.g. child:bike, adult:car).

Cognitive Domain (vertical, left side, with up/down arrow)

← **Social Domain** →

(one-on-one ———→ whole group)

Cloze Procedure

The *cloze* (a shortening of the word *closure*) procedure requires a reader to supply deleted words in a passage using syntactic and/or semantic clues. The student is given a written passage with missing words, and the student supplies the words based on context and passage comprehension. A traditional cloze passage omits every fifth word; however, every fifth to every ninth word may be omitted, using the same omission pattern throughout the passage. The fewer words that are removed, the less challenging the passage is to complete. A traditional cloze passage requires the student to provide the exact word that has been struck from the text. For English learners, a word that makes sense may be considered a correct response. This procedure should be used with a student who is capable of reading for comprehension, rather than a student at the decoding level.

Cloze passages are very adaptable. For example, a category of words such as verbs, nouns, or adverbs may be omitted from the passage. Content words may be omitted to focus student attention on meaning. The following are examples of cloze passages:

Sample Cloze Passage

Missing verbs:

I ___ for a walk on the beach. I ___ shells, seaweed, and sand castles. I ___ in the waves.

Missing content words:

Riding my bike is ___! I can ride all around the ___ by myself. Sometimes my dad lets me ride to the ___ to play with my ___.

Results can be used to help the teacher establish a student's comprehension and suitable reading level. The cloze procedure "has proved to be a useful device for matching both L1 [primary language] and L2 [second language] students with text" (Gunderson 2009, 57). Additionally, it is an excellent strategy to help students build comprehension, especially when discussion and clarification of the student's word choices occurs with the teacher (Gunning 2013).

Various cloze passages should be prepared at a range of levels of text difficulty to help the teacher establish the student's reading level. The passages should be a length suitable for the grade level, and the first and last sentences should be left intact. Passages that use standard English, rather than idiomatic expressions or slang, should be used. Because cloze passages rely heavily on background knowledge, selections should be from culture-neutral text.

The cloze procedure indicates how readable texts are for students. It does not assess a student's particular strengths and weaknesses. Other measures such as running records and reading inventories may be used for diagnostic purposes (Gunderson 2009). Figure 3.6 presents suggested scores for English learners to help teachers make decisions about the student's appropriate reading level (Gunderson 2009).

Figure 3.6 Suggested Cloze Scoring for English Learners

Independent	Instructional	Frustration
70%+	50%–69%	49% or less

Maze Procedure

Similar to the cloze procedure, a *maze* passage provides a student with three or four word choices. While shifting the focus from constructing meaning to recognizing meaning, it provides a scaffold for English language learners. A maze passage can lessen the frustration that English learners may experience in attempting to come up with a word on their own. It can also be a good starting point in building up to a cloze passage (Gunning 2013). As with a cloze passage, the length of a maze passage should be appropriate for the grade or estimated reading level. The word choices should include the correct word, an incorrect word that is the same part of speech, and an incorrect word that is a different part of speech. Figure 3.7 shows a suggested scoring system (Gunderson 2009) followed by an example of a maze passage.

Figure 3.7 Suggested Maze Scoring

Independent	Instructional	Frustration
80% and above	51%–79%	50% or less

Sample Maze Passage

Robin Hood became an outlaw. That is why he went to Sherwood Forest. It was his ____ (sing, shoe, home) for many years. There was a price on his head. It was a reward. It would be given to the ____ (run, dog, man) who would bring him into town.

Robin Hood stayed ____ (hidden, chair, beautiful). He was in the woods ____ (at, for, hop) one year. Other men gathered around him. Each one had been outlawed. In that year, about one hundred good, strong men joined him. They chose him to be their leader.

(Pyle 2013)

Retellings

A retelling is a written or spoken recollection of what a student remembers after reading or listening to a piece of text. It is a type of performance assessment that requires the student to construct a response and engage in higher-order thinking. It is also considered an authentic assessment activity because we commonly engage in retellings when we share our experiences with others.

Retellings indicate what a student

- remembers;
- thinks is important to include;
- can infer from the text; and
- connects from the text to his or her own experiences.

Retellings also indicate how a student

- uses language;
- constructs meaning;
- sequences and organizes information; and
- processes and connects large pieces of text.

A retelling can indicate a student's ease of expression either orally or in writing, and it documents a student's present level of competence. In addition to being an excellent assessment tool, a retelling is an excellent instructional tool. The use of retellings over time helps students improve reading comprehension, concept of story structure, vocabulary, and writing conventions.

A retelling is highly flexible:

- The student can listen to or read a piece of text either in English or in the primary language.
- The student can then perform the retelling either in English or in the primary language. A primary language retelling, if the teacher has a means to assess it, can help determine what primary language resources the student can draw on in support of learning English.
- The student can read the text or listen to someone else read the text, and then perform the retelling either orally or in writing.
- A retelling can be conducted with a teacher, a classroom assistant, a fellow student, or a cross–age helper.

Given the many benefits and the ease and flexibility of doing a retelling, it is an essential tool for assessing English learners, as well as a highly beneficial tool for instructional purposes when used repeatedly.

The following teaching vignette describes the experience of two graduate students, Jamie and Laurie, both elementary teachers, who implemented an action research project based on a creative use of written retellings and buddy journals to assess their English learners and to help all students (fluent English speakers and English learners) improve their reading comprehension and writing skills.

Jamie and Laurie taught third grade at the same school. They wanted to improve their students' text-based comprehension, writing strategies and applications, and writing conventions. They designed an action research project that involved the use of buddy journals and retellings to achieve their goal. Their students included native English speakers and English learners. They decided to partner their students across their two classes and pair a native English speaker with an English learner.

Each student maintained a journal. Twice a week, the students would write to each other. The first entry of the week was on a topic of their choosing. The second entry was a story that their teachers read to them from their reading program. Students then wrote a retelling of the story for their journal buddy to read.

After the students had written an entry, each teacher bundled up the journals, exchanged them, and distributed them to the students' writing buddies in the other classroom. The buddies would write back, and the teachers would again exchange the journals, returning them to the owners who would read and respond to what the buddies had written, whether to an open topic or a retelling of the story that the students had been read. This process meant that the students experienced three exposures to each story: hearing it read, rewriting it, and reading their buddy's retelling.

Jamie and Laurie tracked their students' progress on their written retellings, assessing the retellings based on their own modification of the retelling rubric (see Figure 3.8). They found that assessment of the retelling over a five-week period revealed growth and areas of individual need as well as areas of need for the students as a whole, particularly text-based comprehension.

They concluded that using the retelling assessment for the students' journal writing provided valuable information not only about their students' growth and needs, but also about their own teaching and the need to continue to stress reading comprehension.

Figure 3.8 shows the retelling rubric, which can be used just as it appears. It can also be modified to suit particular teaching and learning needs, as Jamie and Laurie did. Because they wanted to focus on writing conventions, they expanded the "Language Use" section by separating capitalization and punctuation, and added a line that they labeled "complex sentences." A full-size version of the rubric is located in Appendix D.

Figure 3.8 Retelling Rubric

Appendix D • Teacher Resources

Retelling Rubric

Student: _____

Text: _____

Check one:

Text was read aloud to student.
Text was read aloud by student.
Text was read silently by student.
Text was read aloud with student partner.

Other notes or information:

Printed with permission from Zuñiga Dunlap 2006

248

Appendix D • Teacher Resources

Retelling Rubric *(cont.)*

Text recall of . . .	0	1	2	3	4
Sequence					
Main idea(s)					
Supporting ideas					
Important information					
Language Use					
Vocabulary					
Sentence structure (grammar)					
Capitalization and punctuation					
Spelling					
Text Response or Reaction					
Personal observations					
Creative impressions					
Text extension					
Connections across text					

Scoring:

0	No evidence
1	Limited evidence
2	Moderate evidence
3	Substantial evidence
4	Excellent

247

Figure 3.9 is a retelling of Steven Kellogg's version of "Chicken Little" from a fourth grader who was assessed on a standardized test at the intermediate level. She heard the story read aloud and then was asked to write a retelling of it. How would you assess this retelling using the retelling rubric? How could this information help guide your instruction for her?

Figure 3.9 Retelling Example

---

chicken littrer (original work)

Wons Ther was a fox that wonted to it alot av chickens. forst he wanted to it chicken litte we trod a coconut to wem chicken litte sed The shcai is foling. chicken litte told a chicken then ald av The chickens No Thei sed cold The polic. bot The polic ditent cime then The fox drest laik a polis. he sed get en my Trox almost al the chickins got on The Trox chicken litte sed hes The fox The fox got chicken littel and hi pot hem en The Trox The fox sed ai trowd a xoxonat en Yor hed end yo ToT That The scai wos foling a polic ofesor was en a halexopter The fox Trowd the coconat to The scai end la coconat het The walecapter The halexapter fald.

---

chicken littrer [Chicken Little] (interpretation)

wons [once] Ther [there] was a fox that wanted to it [eat] a lot av [of] chickens. forst [first] he wanted to it [eat] Chicken Little. We [he] trowd [throwed = threw] a coconat [coconut =acorn] to wem [him] chicken Little said the sky is falling. Chicken Little told a chicken then al av [all of] the chickens. No thei sed [they said] cold [call] the polic [police] bot [but] the polic dident cime [didn't come.] Then the fox drest [dressed] laik a polis [like a police.] he sed [said] get en [in] my trox [truck] almost al [all] the chickins got on the trox [truck] chicken litte sed [said] hes [he's] the fox The fox got chicken lettel and hi [he] pot [put] hem[him] en [in] the Trox [truck] The fox sed [said] ai [I] trowd [trowed = threw] a xoxonat [coconut = acorn] en[on] ror [your] hed [head] end [and] yu [you] tot [thought] That the sxai [sky] wos [was] faling [falling] a polic [police] ofesor [officer] wos [was] en [in] a helexopter [helicopter] The fox trowd [trowd = threw] the coconat [coconut] to the scai [sky] end [and] la coconat het [the coconut hit] the walecapter [helicopter] the halexapter fald [helicopter fell.]

Writing to Describe a Picture

As with an oral description, a student may be asked to write a story based on a picture that lends itself to using a great deal of language, such as a picture of people engaged in a variety of activities. Recall that Figure 3.2 is a useful resource because it depicts many people engaged in many types of activities. Figure 3.10 is a holistic writing rubric for assessing English language learners' writing. It considers writing fluency and ease of expression, use of vocabulary, grammar, sentence variety, and language mechanics. See Appendix D for a full-size version of the holistic writing rubric.

Figure 3.10 Holistic Writing Rubric for English Learners

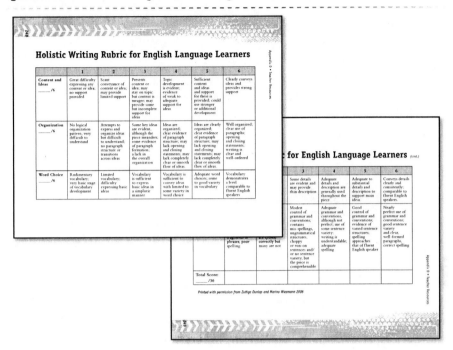

This rubric can be used as a general assessment for students at all writing levels. Assessments that accomapny English learner programs, such as *E.L. Achieve* (http://www.el.achieve.org) should be used to pinpoint a student's precise academic writing needs. This writing rubric may be used to assess a student's repsonse to a writing prompt two or three times throughout the academic year. It may also be used to assess content area writing as well as narrative descriptive writing.

Summary

It is important to maintain a sensible approach to assessment with English learners so that they do not become overwhelmed by the process, nor frustrated with language assessment that is far beyond their abilities.

Another aspect of assessment involves helping English language learners understand the skills and abilities they need to learn to be academically successful. Students should understand, as appropriate for their age and grade, that teaching and learning is a partnership in achieving positive outcomes. Discussing assessment results with students helps them develop learning goals and think intentionally about what they can do to achieve those goals. Long-term English language learners in particular need "invitation, support, and insistence that they become active participants in their own education" (Olsen 2010, 33).

When students and teachers can track progress, everyone gains a sense of accomplishment. Assessment is the way to demonstrate the progress that is being made.

Apply, Reflect, and Extend

1. How do your school and school district track English learners' progress?

2. What resources are available to help assess your students' primary language abilities?

3. Considering the classroom-based assessments in this chapter, which ones would provide you with helpful supplemental information?

4. How might you adapt the retelling rubric to suit your students' needs?

The frustration the listener would experience during this phone conversation mirrors the feelings an English learner can experience. Comprehension during face-to-face conversations can be facilitated by hand gestures and facial expressions. Aspects of language that facilitate understanding can include salient and emphasized words and phrases in a flow of speech, those that are frequently repeated, those that carry clear meanings, or a combination of these. Common language patterns can be another important source to promote listening comprehension. Two examples of language patterns that speakers learn early on are using no to indicate negation, and adding *-ing* or *-ed* to verbs to mark ongoing or past action. To continue the phone analogy, as the reception gets clearer, more words and phrases become comprehensible, and increasingly larger "pieces" of language begin to make sense.

The Importance of Listening and Speaking Skills

Listening and speaking are fundamental life skills that we use every day. They are the essence of daily communication. The Common Core State Standards for English Language Arts Speaking and Listening (2010) require students to go beyond casual conversations and even common verbal classroom engagement techniques such as think-pair-share or heads–together activities. The standards require students to

- hold thoughtful, reflective, sustained academic conversations that may require advance preparation;
- come to class appropriately prepared to participate in such conversations;
- build on existing conversation by adding comments, and asking and responding to questions;
- evaluate a speaker's point of view;
- match speech to the circumstance by using the appropriate register;
- evaluate and synthesize information; and
- make multimedia presentations sourced and synthesized from a variety of materials.

Developing Listening and Speaking Abilities

Chapter 4

Anticipatory Quiz

Are the following statements true or false?

_____ **1.** English learners who receive sufficient meaningful input through everyday exposure to English do not need ELD/ESL instruction.

_____ **2.** Literacy development is based on proficient listening and speaking abilities.

_____ **3.** Learning language patterns and structures is helpful, but meaningful language input is more beneficial.

_____ **4.** Narrow reading, rather than broad reading, is beneficial in promoting listening and speaking for English learners.

_____ **5.** Promoting academic thinking and conversation should be addressed at the later stages of English language development.

Imagine waiting for a phone call concerning an important matter. The phone finally rings. However, the reception is bad, so only certain phrases come through. It starts to sound something like "… told me that …" "… have to do is …" "… in the …" "… you can't …" "… by tomorrow …"

Listening and speaking abilities form the very basis of literacy development, as research supports:

- "Listening and speaking are key foundations of second-language acquisition" (Snow and Katz 2010, 113).

- "Language proficiency is a precursor for effective reading comprehension" (Echevarría, Vogt, and Short 2012, 149).

- "Oral proficiency in English is associated with English reading comprehension and writing skills.... Extensive oral English development must be incorporated into successful literacy instruction" (August and Shanahan 2006, 4).

Interestingly, and unfortunately, listening and particularly speaking are also the very domains of language that are often not given sufficient developmental support or instruction (August and Shanahan 2006). Many studies show that teachers do significant amounts of talking: "on average, 80 percent of all the talking across various activities" (Wasik and Iannone-Campbell 2012, 323). Another study reported that only five minutes of instructional time per day was devoted to activities that develop oral language skills (Cunningham et al. 2009). Students need to have conversations and opportunities to discuss, express ideas, and use vocabulary in academic conversational settings. Along with this goes wait time—sufficient time to develop one's thoughts, and for English learners, to figure out how to express those thoughts in another language.

The following sections describe four established concepts about teaching listening and speaking abilities to English learners.

Abundant and High-Quality Verbal Interactions

Abundant and high-quality experiences in language-rich classrooms with frequent opportunities to hear meaningful language, and engaging in producing language for real communication purposes, provide students with opportunities to hear language models. Through focused give and take, conversation creates the need to formulate responses and negotiate meaning. Hearing English in the classroom exposes students to words and concepts they would not be able to read on their own or hear in casual conversations with friends. English learners need opportunities for discussion based on activities like sorting, ordering, classifying, and organizing, accompanied by verbal negotiated meaning. They need opportunities to craft responses with sufficient think time before being required to answer. Classroom discussion should be based on a variety of experiences that include talking about content-area instruction, informational books, fiction, and poetry, and discussing charts, graphs, maps, and other types of data.

Explicit and Direct Instruction on Grammar and Usage

Regularly scheduled direct instruction from a standardized and complete ELD/ESL scope and sequence curriculum that focuses on all the necessary aspects of grammar and English language usage is essential for English learners. This type of instruction should occur during a designated block of time during the school day (Saunders and Goldenberg 2010). Students should first be assessed on their oral-language proficiency. This is typically accomplished by a standardized state or district-wide test to determine the students' level of language ability. Then, students should be grouped for instruction based on their assessed needs. They should have repeated opportunities to practice and receive corrective instructional feedback. This focused ELD/ESL instruction should be in addition to language experiences woven throughout the rest of the school day's standard academic curriculum. Focused English language support should continue beyond the intermediate stages of conversational ease in order to ensure support and guidance in more refined, academic uses of language.

Focused Teaching of Patterns and Structures

Patterns and structures form the basis of language learning. These can be found at all levels of language, from sound patterns of individual words to grammatical sentence patterns, or structures that support large pieces of discourse. No matter what the language goal, attending to patterns and structures is a critical component of language learning.

Developing listening comprehension initially hinges on discerning how words and phrases are used and attending to grammatical patterns that govern increasingly larger discourse segments. Actively pointing out patterns and structures helps English language learners develop listening and speaking skills.

Construct-Based Instruction

Constructs are guidelines that give structure and form. They help teachers plan for instruction and direct learning outcomes. Three constructs are suggested to help teachers build their listening and speaking development instruction. These constructs are discussed in the next sections, along with teaching strategies and approaches that support their implementation:

- Provide opportunities for students to **listen first and talk later**.

- Help students **build background knowledge and vocabulary** through discussion and repeated exposure to important concepts.

- **Promote academic thinking** that supports academic conversation.

The order of these three constructs does not reflect a progression through which English learners pass. Teachers should use strategies and approaches from all three constructs right from the beginning in all aspects of instruction. The third construct, promoting academic thinking through academic conversations, is the foundation of the CCSS Speaking and Listening Anchor Standards, and teachers should encourage it even from the beginning stages of English language development.

Listen First, Talk Later

Listening first and talking later helps English learners develop conceptual knowledge and vocabulary, and the confidence to begin to use these words. Here are some strategies to help teachers implement this construct.

Comparing Notes

This strategy builds listening and speaking skills through focused listening, synthesizing, and summarizing, with help and collaboration from other students. The process begins with the teacher selecting a piece of text and reading it aloud. The amount of text should be appropriate for both the level of oral proficiency and the age of the students. First, students just listen at least two times to the teacher reading the text aloud. On a subsequent repeated reading, the students write down as many key vocabulary words and important phrases as they can. Then, students pair up to compare notes and combine their efforts. This process gives students an opportunity to discuss and rewrite the material. Pairs then come together to form a group of four. Again, students compare notes and collectively write their re-creation of the text. Students then read their versions aloud. Class members decide whose version comes closest to capturing the text's intent and main ideas (Gunning 2013).

Front-Loading and Advance Cuing

These strategies encourage active listening by placing the important information (front-loading) or questions (advance cuing) in front of the lesson. They are a form of "prelistening." These approaches help listeners know where to focus their attention. They provide aural guideposts and markers to get oriented and stay connected. Just as with reading for a purpose, setting a purpose for listening is effective. In setting listening expectations, it is also important to follow up and hold students accountable for responding.

One Looks, One Doesn't

The principal idea in this strategy is to listen carefully and follow directions. Beginning with foam shapes or colored blocks is a good possibility once students know the names of colors, shapes, and basic prepositional phrases such as *on top of, next to, to the right of,* and *to the left of.* The teacher or another student can be the "describer" who explains where to place the shapes or blocks. The listener, who relies only on verbal guidelines, follows the directions. A book or divider can be placed between the students. The describer should simultaneously lay out the pattern he or she is describing. Then, at the end of the process, the divider can be removed and the describer and the listener can compare to see how closely the listener's pattern matches the describer's explanation (Peregoy and Boyle 2013). The following is an example of One Looks, One Doesn't.

Sample One Looks, One Doesn't

Put down an orange square.

Put a blue triangle to the right of the orange square.

Put a purple circle on top of the orange square.

Put a red rectangle to the left of the orange square.

This type of activity helps students develop careful listening skills, with immediate feedback to assess how well they are able to follow directions.

Oral Retellings

A retelling is a postreading or postlistening recall after having read or listened to a piece of text. Used over time, retellings help develop comprehension because they actively engage the student in recalling text. They can reveal a student's connections and inferences across pieces of text, and reveal how a student processes and reorganizes text. They can also indicate a student's growing ease of oral expression and understanding of characters, setting, plot, and vocabulary. Chapter 3 contains a retelling rubric.

Pairings

This strategy pairs a beginning to intermediate English speaker with a fluent English speaker. Both are assigned the same role or responsibility in a small group. For example, in an expert jigsaw, the two students remain together during the entire process, from the "home" group to the "expert" group. This allows the English learner to participate while listening first, without being directly and fully responsible. It models academic language and allows for multiple passes at the material. Another good use for pairing is a literature circle. This is more effective with intermediate to early advanced English speakers who have developed some reading ability. Pairings can allow for ear-to-ear reading, discussing plot and characters, and clarifying "fuzzy" parts the English learner has encountered. These conversations can occur prior to the literature circle discussion, giving front-loaded information and multiple passes at the material prior to the group discussion.

Show, Tell, and Tell

Knowing in advance that students will be required to respond in some way motivates more focused listening. Before individual sharing or show and tell, students are told that they will be asked to describe or retell what was shared. This promotes active listening and holds students responsible for retelling what they heard.

Virtual Language Experience Approach

Roach Van Allen (1964) developed a comprehensive language arts strategy for the primary grades to promote listening and speaking, and learning to read and write. The essential idea was for children to have a shared experience, such as might be experienced on a class field trip, and return to the classroom to discuss the experience. The teacher would then synthesize the students' language, and the class would write a collective story about their experience, with the teacher serving as the scribe. The students could then take copies of the story to cut into words and sentences to practice reading, find common letters (onsets and rimes), place sentence strips together to re-create the story, and do myriad other language-based activities. Van Allen posed that this language experience approach (LEA) was a powerful way for students to make connections between spoken and written language, and among thought and spoken and written language.

Extending this basic idea to include virtual field trips is an excellent strategy for English learners. The teacher can provide a preview of the "trip," discussing key vocabulary and concepts that the students will encounter. The teacher can serve as a docent through the field trip, stopping to explain or to invite students to pose their questions and offer comments. Students may also write down questions on sticky notes during the field trip, to be discussed afterward (Blachowicz and Obrochta 2005).

Build Background Knowledge and Vocabulary

Listening, repeated exposure, and discussion allow for building background knowledge, developing conceptual understanding, and increasing active listening for important words and phrases. Here are some strategies to help teachers implement this construct.

Narrow Reading

Stephen Krashen (2004) suggests that reading books on similar topics and series books by the same author exposes students to similar vocabulary and related concepts, and in the case of fiction, similar story lines, structures, and characters who encounter similar situations. Narrow reading on any given topic offers multiple opportunities to hear the relevant words and phrases repeatedly (e.g., *chrysalis*, *cocoon*, and *transform* in narrow reading about butterflies). These multiple passes help students build background knowledge, new vocabulary, and concepts. Combining repeated exposure with discussion helps students embed these words in their memories and helps develop increasingly richer ways of understanding and using the words and concepts (Yopp, Yopp, and Bishop 2009).

Text sets are groups or collections of books that address the same or related topics. Reading text sets is a way to implement narrow reading. Stair-step text sets refer to arranging text sets in increasingly difficult reading levels (Hadaway 2009). They provide a way to promote discussion across students with a range of English language abilities.

Developing interest groups for students offers an ideal way to discuss and share information on their chosen narrow reading topics. The teacher can also provide prompts to help students along in the conversational process. Say, for example, there is a soccer aficionado interest group. The following are possible questions to pose as prompts that weave in verbs and language processing promoted by the Common Core Speaking and Listening Standards (hold conversations that require advance preparation; build on existing conversation by adding comments, and asking and responding to questions; evaluate sources and synthesize information; and draw conclusions). Student responses and engagement are predicated on their level of English language development.

- Which professional soccer team is the best? What evidence do you have?
- What sources did you read to help you decide?
- Are these fair, unbiased sources? How do you know?
- Compare and contrast the top two teams: describe one strength and one weakness of each team.

Chapters 5 and 6 provide discussions and other applications of narrow reading.

Narrow Reading and Academic Conversations

In their work on studying academic conversations with English language learners, Jeff Zwiers and Marie Crawford (2009) suggest six key elements that must be included to take students from simple and superficial to in-depth and sophisticated thinking expressed in academic conversation:

- coming up with a worthy topic

- elaborating and clarifying

- supporting ideas with evidence

- building on and challenging ideas

- applying or connecting

- paraphrasing and summarizing

As with any strategy, students must receive explicit instruction when learning these conversation prompts. Zwiers and Crawford suggest having students practice just one conversational support at a time and memorizing an associated verbal prompt as well as a related hand motion.

In their work, Zwiers and Crawford found that students had to be taught that these strategies or prompts were not a check-off list to get through during a conversation. This helped students develop a sense of the recursive nature of conversations. Eventually, they learned to apply these strategies as the direction of the conversation suggested in order to understand someone's point or to respectfully challenge an idea that was posed.

Zwiers and Crawford found that hand gestures and sentence starters associated with each element helped students remember and guide each other in the academic conversation process. Figure 4.1 outlines these hand gestures and verbal prompts.

Figure 4.1 Conversation Prompts

Conversational Element	Hand Gesture	Verbal Prompts
Coming up with a worthy topic	Fingers and hands forming a rectangle	• Why do you think the author wrote this? • What's an idea that emerged in this?
Elaborating and clarifying	Pulling hands and fingers in opposite directions	• What do you mean by ...? • Can you tell me more about ...? • What makes you think ...?
Supporting ideas with evidence	Fingers of one hand supporting the other hand	• Can you give an example? • Can you show me where it says that?
Building on and challenging ideas	Repeatedly layering hands one on top of the other	• What do you think? • Can you add to this idea? • Do you agree? • What's another point of view?
Applying or connecting	Hooking hands together	• What can we learn from this idea/character? • How can we apply this to our lives?
Paraphrasing and summarizing	Cupping hands together	• What have we discussed so far? • How can we summarize what we've talked about?

The authors reported that this conversational process improved student academic performance. Students began to include supportive evidence in their writing and to use academic vocabulary in responding orally to questions (Zwiers and Crawford 2009). Combining narrow reading with the Zwiers and Crawford guidelines for implementing academic conversations is a powerful strategy for promoting academic conversations for English learners.

Plays, Skits, and Read-Arounds

These types of activities are not about producing on-the-spot speech—rather, they produce rehearsed speech. Nonetheless, repeated reads and memorization are powerful tools to help anchor language in memory that becomes available for future use in conversations. Further, spoken language fluency supports reading fluency, and it also helps students learn the natural rhythms and cadences of spoken English. An added benefit of brief plays and skits is that adding movement to words and phrases is another modality that further helps embed language in memory.

The Stories to Grow By with Whootie Owl website (www.storiestogrowby.com/script_body.html) offers simple reader's theater scripts for groups of students ranging from four to fourteen in number. They are simplified folktales from countries around the world and are based on themes such as loyalty and resourcefulness. Another benefit is that the reader-level range of these reader's theater plays is appropriate for early to intermediate English learners.

Targeted Language Objectives

An important way for teachers to build student awareness, exposure, and repeated use of language is to include a language objective, in addition to a content objective, as part of the daily content curriculum (Echevarría, Vogt, and Short 2012). Here are two examples:

- Count how many transitional words the author uses (e.g., *however, otherwise, besides, conversely,* and *therefore*); use at least one in individual speaking or writing today.

- Record at least five prepositional phrases encountered in today's science reading (e.g., *across Earth, next to rivers,* and *deep inside the cave*).

Promote Academic Thinking

Academic language is embedded in the cognitive processes—reasoning, perception, logical thinking, decision making, problem solving, and language—used to express understanding. The challenge for English learners is that academic language can be abstract, and therefore difficult to put into words. For beginning English language learners, the need resides in making abstract thinking concrete enough to be able to express it simply. Here are some strategies to help teachers implement this construct.

Analogies

Analogies are powerful ways of getting students to engage in thinking about relationships. Asking English learners to identify relationships among basic vocabulary words provides students with simple and concrete ways to express their thinking without the need for extended dialogue.

For example, the teacher lays out four or more pictures of objects. (More than four makes the cognitive task more challenging.) The teacher selects four picture cards with which to form an analogy. The teacher demonstrates thinking about and selecting them on the basis of relationship and category of the objects. The teacher then models the standard analogy verbal pattern, "*X* is to *Y* as *A* is to *B*," while showing and talking about the selected pictures. Showing pictures with the words to express them engages the students in comparing and contrasting while providing a specific language pattern. By selecting the related pictures, rather than producing the language to support the selection, the student engages in thinking (in any language), and then he or she uses a standard and simple language pattern to express category and relationship. Basic vocabulary cards with pictures on one side and words on the other allow for independently practicing the words and the analogies.

Here are some analogies using simple words to get started with:

- bird : nest :: person : house
- pencil : paper :: fingers : keyboard
- bird : feathers :: person : clothes
- hair : person :: feathers : bird
- kitten : cat :: puppy : dog
- book : library :: student : classroom
- ear : head :: fingers : hand
- teeth : mouth :: toes : foot
- butterflies : fly :: fish : swim
- feet : walk :: wings : fly
- red : apple :: yellow : sun

Open Sorts

Another way to express thinking without the need for a great deal of language is by using open sorts. This strategy has students manipulate cards by sorting them into piles for which they themselves have developed their own categories. As with analogy cards, open sorts promote critical thinking while simultaneously employing simple word patterns such as "We use these at lunch" or "We wear these." The teacher can first model selecting a small number of pictures and provide one sentence describing the category. Modeling language for students provides critical listening opportunities and a bridge to making thinking visible. As with analogy cards, pictures can appear on one side of the card with the printed word on the other. This allows students to independently practice with the vocabulary. The number of cards and categories can be adjusted to the level of students' language.

Open sorts offer multiple opportunities for language and meaning negotiation. It is quite possible that students may find different categories from the ones the teacher had in mind, which can demonstrate divergent thinking—an important element in thinking critically.

Open sort cards for beginning English language learners can include objects related to the following:

- classroom
- recess
- lunch
- clothing
- girls' clothing
- boys' clothing
- mammals
- reptiles
- fish

Pictures of unrelated objects or topics may also be used. The following two sets of pictures could be sorted based on a variety of criteria. Just a few examples are habitat, color, and animal classification for the first set of pictures; and groups of people versus individuals, or the type of activity portrayed for the second set of pictures. Asking students to explain their thinking helps them develop vocabulary as well as critical-thinking abilities.

Sort each set of pictures in two different ways. Explain why you grouped them in these ways.

Set 1

Set 2

Semantic Feature Analysis (SFA)

This strategy is another excellent tool for engaging students in critical thinking and academic language. As with analogies and open sorts, SFA provides a structure for students to promote thinking and practice speaking skills. It also provides a pattern or structure that is essential in scaffolding language for English learners. This strategy may be more appropriate for intermediate to advanced English language learners. It requires focused academic student discussion, as emphasized in the Common Core for English Language Arts Speaking and Listening Anchor Standards requiring students to compare and contrast, identify, justify, and support.

This strategy is typically used in conjunction with a unit of study, and it offers opportunities for students to talk about and clarify understanding. The first step is for the teacher to select the most important words and decide on qualities or characteristics they may or may not share. These are placed on a grid: vocabulary words along the side and qualities or characteristics along the top. The teacher and students together decide which features are true or false and indicate this with a plus sign (+) or a minus sign (–), a process that requires focus and discussion. Figure 4.2 shows an example of such a grid, for the story *The Three Little Pigs*.

Figure 4.2 *The Three Little Pigs* Example

	impatient	hardworking	playful	wise	lazy
wolf	+	–	–	–	+
1st pig	+	–	+	–	+
2nd pig	+	–	+	–	+
3rd pig	–	+	–	+	–

"Can you give me an example from the story that shows why the first pig was lazy?" and "What makes you think the third pig was wise?" are just two examples of questions that can prompt discussion and student reference back to the text.

The example shown in Figure 4.3 demonstrates that it is possible to use this strategy for more sophisticated concepts and evaluation of characteristics or qualities. Instead of + and –, here A = Always, N = Never, and S = Sometimes are used.

Figure 4.3 Polygons Example

	plane figure	straight sides	4 sides 4 vertices	4 sides 4 right angles
triangle	A	A	N	N
rectangle	A	A	A	A
octagon	A	A	N	N
parallelogram	A	A	A	S
quadrilateral	A	A	A	S

Summary

Speaking and listening abilities are the fundamental language components that provide the basis for literacy development. Additionally, the Common Core State Standards lay out specific listening and speaking requirements. Therefore, they are necessary language domains to incorporate into the curriculum. Offering abundant opportunities to engage in high-quality listening and speaking activities, providing explicit and direct instruction on grammar and usage, teaching patterns and structures, and incorporating construct-based instruction are essential for promoting and developing oral skills. This chapter outlined many teaching strategies to promote the development of these two important language domains.

Apply, Reflect, and Extend

1. What is your estimation of the amount of time in your classroom that students hold meaningful discussions? How can you gather basic data to check your estimate?

2. Do your students have equal exposure to hearing and discussing fiction and nonfiction texts? Listing the last several read-alouds to your class can help you verify your answer.

3. Select at least one strategy from each of the constructs to adapt to your teaching needs.

Chapter 5

Building Vocabulary

Anticipatory Quiz

Are the following statements true or false?

_____ 1. Fifth or sixth grade is the ideal time for English language learners to begin studying root words, prefixes, and suffixes.

_____ 2. English language learners should be given important vocabulary to learn in advance of a lesson.

_____ 3. Because of their limited exposure to academic language in general, English learners should slowly work their way through memorizing the Academic Word List.

_____ 4. Repetition of vocabulary is unnecessary and boring.

_____ 5. Spanish speakers intuitively make use of Spanish–English cognates.

_____ 6. English language learners should have limited exposure to read-alouds.

_____ 7. While wide reading is advocated for vocabulary development, narrow reading may serve English learners better.

Consider this phrase: "Words are like people. I never met one I didn't like." Beyond a lighthearted comparison, it can be said that in many ways, words are like people, as shown in Figure 5.1.

Figure 5.1 Words Are Like People

Point of Comparison	Meeting People	Learning Words
Repeated experiences	Meeting a person once does not constitute really knowing the individual. The more time spent with the person, the more familiar and known he or she becomes. There are degrees of knowing someone, depending on the circumstance, the nature of the relationship, the frequency of seeing the person, and the circumstances of the interactions. Spending time repeatedly with a person allows for better understanding of who he or she really is.	Words are learned incrementally over time and with increased exposure. Developing depth of understanding and meaning of new vocabulary requires many exposures—ten at a bare minimum to really learn a word. Repeated exposure develops familiarity, which in turn brings sufficient confidence to begin using the word. Only through use can an individual say "I know that word."
Early exposure	The sooner a child starts interacting and socializing with people in meaningful ways, the more he or she learns about them, and the more adept he or she becomes at meeting others and making new friends.	Early exposure to language and concept learning is critical for laying a foundation for vocabulary development.
Building background knowledge	Introducing one friend to another typically involves sharing something interesting about each one in order to build a connection or a social bridge between them.	Building background knowledge is essential for vocabulary development. It helps to form mental connections among words and concepts, and helps solidify understanding.

Point of Comparison	Meeting People	Learning Words
Forming new relationships	Hearing about someone, being familiar with his or her line of work, knowing a family member, or learning that there is a shared common interest, helps a person understand something about that individual even before meeting him or her. Background knowledge about someone is useful in helping develop a relationship. The more background knowledge you have about a person, the easier it is to anchor that person in some way in the memory.	Background knowledge is critical in learning new words and related concepts, as it provides mental anchors for new information. Adding new vocabulary to familiar concepts helps organize, structure, categorize, and integrate new and familiar concepts and words.
Active engagement	Simply sitting on the sidelines watching others is not the way to get to know people. Active involvement and engagement, and shared experiences, facilitate relationship building.	The best way to learn words is to actively engage in using and applying them.
Applying strategies	Developing social skills and strategies for meeting and talking to people makes it easier to interact with new people that you meet.	Direct and explicit instruction is required in order to learn how to use and apply word-learning strategies.
Context	Context greatly affects how we interact with others. We have colleagues and professional friends, family friends, close friends, and weekend hanging-out friends, all of whom we see for a variety of purposes and occasions.	Words serve different purposes and are used in different contexts. Some words are appropriate for social language. Others are appropriate for reading academic content. Yet other words give us directions to follow. Still other words are used only in context-specific situations. We have to learn to use a variety of words, and use them in the appropriate circumstances.

Point of Comparison	Meeting People	Learning Words
Careful selection	You can't get to know too many people at one time. This causes confusion, and you might forget their faces, their names, where they are from, and other important information about them.	Do not overload teaching and learning with too many words! Teaching a wise and careful selection of a small number of important words is much more effective than trying to teach too many.
New opportunities	Meeting new people can add new dimensions to your life.	Being curious about words is an effective way to build vocabulary.
Building close relationships	Getting to know someone well means that person becomes part of your life. You spend time with the person and enjoy experiences together. You may seek help and advice from him or her. You rely on that person.	The goal of learning words is not just to recognize them, but to use them as a part of daily life.

Figure 5.1 describes established concepts about vocabulary development that hold true for learning vocabulary in one's native language as well as in a new language. However, are there differences? Are there aspects of vocabulary development in learning English as a second language that a teacher should pay more attention to than others? The answer to both questions is yes. The following sections explore these aspects under nine key topics:

- building background knowledge
- using explicit, direct, and systematic instruction
- developing spelling skills
- carefully selecting vocabulary
- using nonlinguistic representations of vocabulary
- using repetition and multiple exposures
- teaching students strategies to help themselves
- using read-alouds
- applying narrow reading

Building Background Knowledge

One of the biggest challenges any student faces is learning new vocabulary. This is especially true for English learners. The most challenging task of all is learning new vocabulary along with the ideas that support it (Gunning 2013). For students who come from limited backgrounds and experiences, and who are also English learners, the simultaneous tasks of building background knowledge and building vocabulary in a second language are indeed daunting. The following sections outline a variety of ways that teachers of English language learners can help their students develop background knowledge.

Assessment in Planning for Instruction

Making pre-assessments of students' vocabulary prior to instruction is a good practice. One way is to select nine important words or phrases. Place them in chart form (see Figure 5.2). It is important to add a sentence or phrase for context. The students' textbook can serve as a resource to make use of graphics, charts, and other available information for focused searches. Students can complete the chart in pairs or small groups, which helps promote discussion and shared knowledge about the meaning of the words. Primary language can be used in completing this task, including online translation resources to provide an understanding of the key concepts and important words. However, two cautions should be mentioned here. First, while translations convey the important ideas, they are not always exactly grammatically correct. Second, students must eventually learn to negotiate their own meanings and to express them in their own words. Reading translations of other people's words does not provide active learning. Active engagement in learning vocabulary is the best teacher.

The following vocabulary pre-assessment/background builder is an example that might be used to support teaching Next Generation Science Standards' Disciplinary Core Idea: MS-LS2 Ecosystems: Interaction, Energy, and Dynamics.

Figure 5.2 Sample Vocabulary Pre-assessment/Background Builder

	Here is what this word or phrase means: (in my language) (in a drawing) (in an English phrase)	We have seen this word or phrase and it might mean something like . . .	We have seen this word or phrase, but we are not sure what it means.	Here is our own sentence using this word.
ecosystem An ecosystem is a community of living things and the environment needed to live together.				
resource A resource occurs in nature and is needed for living things to survive.				
interdependence Sticking together because we need each other means that we are interdependent.				
matter Matter is made up of everything around us that takes up space.				

	Here is what this word or phrase means: (in my language) (in a drawing) (in an English phrase)	We have seen this word or phrase and it might mean something like . . .	We have seen this word or phrase, but we are not sure what it means.	Here is our own sentence using this word.
energy Energy gives any living thing the ability to move and do work.				
cycle Many steps that happen over and over again create a cycle.				
dynamic Action, force, and energy make dynamic movement.				
biodiversity Many types of plants and animals create biodiversity.				
resilience "Taking a hit" and bouncing back means that you are resilient.				

This type of background builder helps English language learners begin to actively search for important content words and phrases in text, and build information about what these words and phrases mean. This activity is also helpful for teachers to assess what students may already know. It might also be used as a follow-up assessment.

Leveled Readers

An important way to ease students into topics and to introduce vocabulary and concepts without overwhelming students is through the use of leveled readers. Matching reading material to the student's reading ability serves to build reading confidence and teach, clarify, or reinforce vocabulary. Consider just some of the vocabulary opportunities taken from a leveled reader whose story includes decodable words that contain the long *e* sound: *beast, breeze, creek, creepy, flee, peeked*, and *squeak*. A student's repeated reads of this story can teach and reinforce new words while also, in this case, reinforcing the long *e* sound.

Pictorial Input Chart

A Pictorial Input Chart is one of the many highly effective strategies from Project GLAD (Guided Language Acquisition Design), a U.S. Department of Education Academic Excellence Program (Brechtel 2001). This strategy combines the teacher's verbal explanations, accompanied by simultaneous drawings, and written vocabulary, offering strong imprinting with multiple processing modes.

The process works as follows. In advance of an introductory lesson to a unit, the teacher prepares by lightly tracing in pencil a diagram or picture of an important aspect of the unit of study. This can be accomplished by placing a picture on a document camera and tracing it onto a large piece of butcher paper that has been taped to the board. It is important to make the figure large enough for students to see during a whole-class discussion. Examples of what a teacher may decide to trace vary according to imagination and curricular needs, and range from a whale and its organs to a sketch of the Nile River and its geographical and environmental components. The teacher should also pencil in the vocabulary items, ensuring that they are included as labels next to the relevant parts of the penciled sketch. When first sharing and discussing the sketch, the teacher marks over the penciled sketch and vocabulary with colored markers while talking. Thus, the drawing appears to come to life while the teacher is talking to students about it. The teacher can address as much or as little vocabulary as desired on the first day, with the possibility of adding more on subsequent days. The pictorial chart stays up during the entire unit for student reference.

Preview/Review

A long-standing and highly effective strategy, preview/review was initially developed to support students in bilingual classes. This strategy first requires the teacher to select one, two, or a maximum of three of the most important ideas of a lesson. Then, the teacher chooses no more than nine words that are essential for understanding the lesson's key concepts. The teacher determines how best to demonstrate the vocabulary and related meaning to students. The teacher then provides a maximum ten-minute preview for the English learners while English speakers are engaged in a warm-up or anticipatory activity. Asking students to take notes and write down information is also important. This supports oral and written modes of processing the information, and it gives students an opportunity to review the information later on their own. If time permits, the teacher can do a five- to seven-minute review at the end of the lesson. The two most critical aspects of meaningful implementation are

- tightly focusing on the one or two key ideas of the lesson
- selecting no more than nine words that the teacher clearly and visually demonstrates to support student understanding

The following is a preview plus lesson on water tension that was taught exclusively in Spanish to teacher credential students (in the United States) in what the instructor calls a "shoe on the other foot" experience. The intent was to help preservice teachers understand what it is like to have to learn content in a non-native language. Another goal of the lesson was to help teacher credential students process some of the strategies that helped them make sense of the lesson's content, with the idea that they will remember and use these strategies with their own students.

Some of the teacher credential students spoke and wrote Spanish or felt comfortable enough in Spanish to self-select to stay with the few fluent Spanish speakers in the class.

In preparation, the instructor created four open-ended questions for the fluent Spanish-speaking students to get them thinking about water tension.

At the beginning of the lesson, the instructor explained that students would be divided into two groups: Spanish speakers and non–Spanish speakers. To activate discussion and background knowledge, the Spanish speakers discussed and responded in writing to four questions (in Spanish):

1. Why do big drops of water sliding down a window stick together?

2. What happens when you poke a drop of water with a pin or a pencil?

3. Why can some bugs walk on water? Why don't they sink?

4. What are molecules and how do they affect each other?

Meanwhile, the instructor conducted the introductory preview in Spanish with her limited and non-Spanish-speaking students.

The following are the key preview vocabulary words for the non–Spanish speakers:

1. *agua* (water)

2. *gota/gotero* (drop/water dropper)

3. *botella* (bottle)

4. *fuerza* (force)

5. *fuerza invisible* (invisible force)

6. *fuerza cohesive* (cohesive force)

The most challenging to demonstrate is *fuerza* (force), the key concept and vocabulary word, which the instructor showed by making a great effort to push and pull a table, and to show her "muscular" arms. The teacher showed *invisible* (clearly a cognate) by covering her eyes and pushing and pulling at the table. She intertwined her fingers and locked them together to demonstrate cohesive force. She showed students a small bottle, a water dropper (*gotero*), and one drop (*gota*) from the water dropper.

She asked students to copy two sentences:

1. *La fuerza entre moléculas = fuerza cohesive.* (Force between molecules is called cohesive force.)

2. *Moléculas de la misma sustancia tienden pegarse por una fuerza invisible.* (Molecules of the same substance tend to stick together because they are attracted by an invisible force.)

Then all students in the class were placed in small groups to conduct two short experiments, with explanations in Spanish from the instructor, with a great deal of demonstration, and with Spanish speakers and Spanish learners working together. The instructor ensured that at least one member of each group was a Spanish speaker.

The first experiment was to see how many drops of water each group could fit on a penny. There were two attempts. After each attempt, each group reported how many drops they fit, with the process becoming quite competitive. The second experiment was to form large water drops on a piece of wax paper, with the groups seeing how large they could make each drop become before it started to break apart.

As the instructor circulated, she added explanations and asked questions of each group. Then, drawing students together, she asked for their conclusions about the experiments. Essentially students explained, in Spanish, that force between molecules is called *cohesive force*, and molecules of the same substance cohere due to an invisible force.

Here are processing observations from the teacher credential students after the lesson:

1. For some, it took a great deal of focus not to drift away when the language became difficult to understand. Learning in a second language can be difficult.

2. Some said they relied on background knowledge.

3. Some said they were able to use cognates.

4. They relied on the native Spanish speakers to help them broker understanding.

5. The hands-on experiences, slow language, wait time, and especially repetition of terms were very helpful.

Even though this lesson was conducted with adults on an abstract scientific concept, the principles of the preview/review strategy were effective. The observations made by students themselves helped them understand in a personal way strategies that can promote comprehension, as well as the feelings and attitudes that their own students might experience when learning content in a second language.

Preview/review can be done in English or in the primary language of students, if students speak the same primary language. Both possibilities are opportunities to develop background knowledge. Again, online translation resources can assist in conveying the key ideas.

Virtual Field Trips

These activities offer ways to

- build concept knowledge along with related target vocabulary;

- concretely show and explain abstract ideas and processes (e.g., an archeologist discovering an important find at a geological site or a reenactment of a historical event);

- promote active listening and questioning that can be teacher or "docent" mediated;

- support reading and writing activities; and

- be subsequently revisited and reviewed independently by students.

Camille Blachowicz and Connie Obrochta (2005) suggest that asking students to do first writes in preparation for virtual field trips can help students activate knowledge and vocabulary they may already have. These can be used as a pre-assessment and then compared to final writes at the completion of the unit, when students write about the concepts and vocabulary they learned, so students see for themselves how much they have learned by the end of the unit. Group talk is another strategy that can be embedded in virtual field trips. Asking students to form comments and questions at designated stopping points can be very effective as well. Alternatively, students can jot down questions and comments on sticky notes as they proceed through the field trip.

The following websites include virtual field trip resources:

- A Hotlist on Virtual Field Trips: This site includes options for math, science, the arts, and social studies trips (http://www.kn.att.com/wired/fil/pages/listvirtualte.html).

- SMART Board Resources—Virtual Field Trips: This site offers collections of field trips from a variety of sources that address many levels and topics (http://sites.google.com/site/whiteboardmaterials/).

Using Direct, Explicit, and Systematic Instruction

English learners need specific and direct instruction to focus attention on what is important in the sea of language that surrounds them. High-frequency words, academic words, morphemes, and cognates require direct instruction and are discussed in this section.

High-Frequency Words

The first 1,000 words found on most high-frequency lists account for about 84 percent of the words we use in casual conversation, and the top 2,000 words account for about 90 percent (Nation 2001, as cited in Peregoy and Boyle 2013). Often, these words do not follow standard spelling conventions because they are drawn from a wide array of languages with different spelling bases, and many are the oldest words in the language and have been modified over the centuries through frequent use.

Many sources for high-frequency word lists exist. The General Service List, developed in 1953 by Michael West, is a long-standing and respected list of the 2,284 most frequently appearing words in English, listed in order of frequency. As a brief introduction, here are the top ten most frequently used words in English from this list: *the, be, of, and, a, to, in, he, have, it.* The New General Service List is a thorough alphabetical listing of the most important high-frequency words for English learners (Browne, Culligan, and Phillips 2013). The Dolch word list contains 220 high-frequency words. School districts often develop their own high-frequency word lists by grade level.

High-frequency lists include function words and content words. Function words like *to, in, for, at,* and *how* show relationships among words and sentences. These are best taught in the context of printed and spoken language. Content words are concrete and specific, such as *blue, chair, say,* and *see*; their meanings can be demonstrated. For English learners, "high-frequency content words are good candidates for explicit instruction because they pack so much meaning even when presented in isolation" (Peregoy and Boyle 2013, 228). Thomas Gunning (2013), along with other reading experts, suggests that three or four high-frequency words per week is a sufficient number for students to learn, particularly if they are learning academic content-area vocabulary as well.

Academic Vocabulary

Students are expected to understand and use *academic vocabulary* to express concepts and ideas they learn in school. Students encounter academic vocabulary in both oral and written forms. They learn and use this vocabulary in "mutually supportive ways, although … [it is] prevalent in written language in a more concentrated form" (Nagy and Townsend 2012, 92).

William Nagy and Dianna Townsend also state that "the specialized language used in academic settings facilitates communication and thinking about disciplinary content" (2012, 92). Academic vocabulary supports the use of academic language in general because language and thinking are inseparable. Nagy and Townsend observe that "cognitive processing of disciplinary concepts and phenomena would be nearly impossible without academic language" (92). This implies that when students learn the vocabulary of a particular discipline, they are also developing the equally important ability to think like a scientist, a historian, or a mathematician (Bowers and Keisler 2011).

Academic vocabulary is divided into two categories: *general* and *content specific* (also referred to as *discipline specific* or *domain specific*).

General academic words may

- be cross-curriculum words that explain common academic procedures (e.g., *compare, contrast, cite, support,* and *argue*) or functions (e.g., transition words like *additionally, in spite of,* etc.); and

- pertain broadly to all academic disciplines, such as *adverse, characterize,* and *component*. Some general academic words need to be explained in particular contexts, because they carry different meanings that are context dependent. For example, the definition of the word *tension* changes if it is used in the social sciences or in the sciences.

Content-specific words pertain to specific academic domains, such as *allele* and *blastocyst* in biology, or *allophone* and *glottal stop* in linguistics.

Nagy and Townsend (2012) point out that academic vocabulary and academic language in general are challenging for students because they are

- not generally used in informal conversation;

- Latin and Greek based (read about Latin and Greek words and morphology in the section that follows);

- morphologically sophisticated (e.g., *compare, comparable, comparison, incomparable*); and

- abstract, technical, and can be content specific (e.g., *derivation, predisposition, prohibit, extract*).

Many English learners are exposed to academic vocabulary only in school settings, and possibly through their own independent reading. Therefore, academic words are essential to include in direct, explicit, and systematic instruction because they provide a gateway to school success. Further, the Common Core State Standards abound with academic procedural vocabulary (*analyze, integrate, evaluate,* etc.). Students require a great deal of direct engagement with this vocabulary and repeated opportunities to apply them to classroom tasks.

Joshua Lawrence, Claire White, and Catherine Snow (2010) describe a successful cross-curricular academic vocabulary development program for middle school students called Word Generation (http://www.wg.serpmedia.org). This five-day program, Monday through Friday, engages students in using selected academic words while discussing controversial topics such as whether or not there should be grade requirements to play on sports teams. Throughout the week, students are given opportunities for repeated exposure to the vocabulary and ample opportunities to use these words in oral and written forms. Students are supported in academic thinking, speaking, and writing. The program's website includes useful teaching resources and videos of students at work in classrooms engaged with academic vocabulary. The discussions and debates that students hold around controversial topics prepare them well for the argumentative writing requirements of the Common Core.

The Academic Word List (AWL), developed by Averil Coxhead (2000), is a list of 570 root words (or head words) that are the most commonly used in college-level textbooks, drawn from the areas of the arts, commerce, law, and science. These root words plus their affixes are called *word families*. An example is *benefit* (root word), and *beneficial, beneficiary, beneficiaries, benefitted, benefitting,* and *benefits* (word family). The list includes process words and content words, with some examples shown in Figure 5.3.

Figure 5.3 Examples of AWL Process Words and Content Words

Process Words (Verbs)	Content Words (Nouns)
assess	attitude
contrast	device
conclude	component
enable	tradition
exclude	compound

While Coxhead's AWL is a helpful resource for all students, it is drawn from college-level textbooks. (The AWL, along with a comparison of other word lists, appears in Appendix D of this book.) Coxhead recommends that students learn academic words as they arise in the context of their studies. She cautions against teaching these words in alphabetical order and against simultaneously teaching head words that look similar, such as *commence, comment,* and *commit* (Coxhead 2011). She also points out that students must make use of these words, rather than simply learning to spell them and memorizing their meaning. Again, the importance of repeatedly and actively engaging with words in order to truly "own" them is emphasized.

Morphological Awareness, Cognates, and the Need for Direct Instruction

A morpheme is the smallest unit of a language that carries meaning. *Eat*, *speak*, *-ed*, *'s*, and *-ing* are all examples. *Eat* and *speak* are considered root or base words, or free morphemes. Bound morphemes are prefixes and suffixes, and inflected morphemes that are grammatical markers such as *'s* (possession), *-ed* (past tense), and *-ing* (present progressive). The Common Core State Standards expect students as early as the first grade to identify common root words or free morphemes, which carry their own meaning (e.g., *eat*, *speak*, *look*, *use*). By the third grade, students should know and use common prefixes and suffixes. Being able to divide words into meaningful parts—morphemes—is a powerful strategy, and it's essential for English learners.

About 60 percent of English root words and about 75 percent of Spanish root words are derived from Latin (Rasinski et al. 2008). This means that there are a great number of cognates in English and Spanish. Cognates are words that are the same or similar in meaning and sound across languages. Examples from Spanish and English are *opinión* and *opinion*, and *desorientar* and *to disorient*. Many resources for teachers of English learners indicate that pointing out cognates to Spanish speakers who are learning English can be useful. It is true that knowledge of cognates can transfer across languages and can be helpful in figuring out meaning across languages. Research findings show that Spanish speakers' knowledge of root words and affixes is a good predictor of vocabulary development in English (Dressler et al. 2011; Ramirez, Chen, and Pasquarella 2013). In fact, helping students develop and learn to apply English language morphological awareness in general provides "multiple important roles in English reading comprehension for students [not just in Spanish but] from a variety of home language backgrounds" (Kieffer and Lesaux 2012, 1170). These languages are quite varied, as the following list indicates:

- Arabic (Saiegh-Haddad and Geva 2008)
- Chinese (Zhang et al. 2010)
- French (Deacon, Wade-Woolley, and Kirby 2007)
- Hebrew (Schiff and Calif 2007)
- Korean (Wang, Ko, and Choi 2009)

- Spanish (Kieffer and Lesaux 2008; Ramirez, Chen, and Pasquarella 2013)

- Vietnamese (Kieffer and Lesaux 2012)

However, there is a critical point that teachers must be aware of and address when it comes to using knowledge of cognates and morphemes: students do not intuitively or automatically apply word knowledge in general, or specific primary language knowledge, to help them understand cognates. It is not sufficient to point out specific cognates, root words, or affixes; or provide students with lists of cognates and root words; or tell students to look for them as they read. These approaches fall short of teaching students the language knowledge they need to begin to make use of cognates and morphology as meaning-making strategies. Teachers of English learners need to put into practice five essential strategies regarding cognates:

- Point out words that are cognates, root words, and affixes that carry cross-language meaning.

- Offer direct instruction on seeking out and using knowledge of root words and affixes in English.

- Provide students with repeated opportunities to seek and find cognates, root words, and affixes to discover their meaning when they read.

- Review and continually use the cognates and affixes students have studied, and ask students to do the same, in order to reinforce their meanings.

- Help students obtain meaning with cognates that are embedded in text (Kieffer and Lesaux 2012).

Just as with any other strategy that teachers want students to apply consistently and effectively, students must have opportunities for repeated practice with cognates. By actively and continually seeking out similarities in English and the home languages that use Latin- and Greek-based words, and by learning to apply morphological "clues," students can apply their knowledge in breaking apart and understanding words in English, and can therefore improve vocabulary and reading comprehension (Kieffer and Lesaux 2012; Ramirez, Chen, and Pasquarella 2013).

How can teachers do this? Creating an interest in words, or creating word consciousness, is the key to helping students begin to see cross-linguistic relationships and morphological structures. Also, systematically tracking the words assists in revisiting them because recycling and revisiting words is an essential part of learning new vocabulary and deepening meanings of words. The following is an application example of the points just outlined. It describes a lesson that shows how a teacher might take selected words from a read-aloud as they are encountered along the way. It is an example of the point that Michael Kieffer and Nonie Leseaux (2012) make: help students obtain meaning from words that are embedded in text. The lesson is useful for both English learners and fluent English speakers.

Boys and girls, as you know, we are reading *Pippi Longstocking* together. I want to share this paragraph on the second page that I've read aloud to you. Look carefully at the words I have underlined (*captain, disappeared, floated*). Do you know that these words have travelled very far and over many, many centuries to appear in this book, and in the English language? These words also exist in other languages. We call words that are the same or similar in meaning and sound across languages *cognates*. So, for example, *captain*, *capitán* in Spanish, and *capitaine* in French are cognates. Do any of you know words that look or sound anything like *disappear* and *float* in another language? (Spanish: *desaparecer, flotar*)

Let's just think about the word *disappear* today. Can any of you guess which language this word came from—and when? It is a French word and it began to be used—it appeared—in the fifteenth century! Can you divide this word? How can we divide it? Yes, *dis* and *appear*. Who remembers what *dis-* means? Yes, *apart* or *away*, or an opposite force. How about *appear*? Yes, to show up, to come in to sight, to be visible. So, *disappear* means to be apart or away from sight.

Now, this week we are going to look for all the *dis-* words we can find and write them here to keep track of them. How many do you predict we'll find? Let's see who can come the closest to predicting the number that we'll find. For the moment, I want us to get back to the word *disappear* and think of all the words we can right now that use *disappear* or *desaparecer* as a base or root word, both in English and in Spanish. We can add to them as we think of them this week.

English	Spanish
disappear	desaparecer
	desaparezco
	desaparecen
	desaparaces
disappears	desaparece
disappeared	desapareció
	desapareciste
	desaparecidos
	desaparecidas
	desapareciéron
disappearing	desapareciendo

Now, let's read out loud all together these three sentences that are around the word *disappeared* and that include *disappeared* so that you can hear the word read in its context as part of the story.

This type of lesson is an ideal introduction for engaging students in word sorts in which they practice forming words with *dis-* and a variety of root words.

As another lesson example, prepare 3" × 5" cards, eight with *dis-* written on them and ten with root words (e.g., *qualify, honest, agree, cold, true, ability, appoint, approve, comfort, connect*). Have students create words with these cards by placing the cards together, but tell them that two words will be left over because two of them cannot be used with *dis-*. Can they guess which ones will be left over? Can they figure out what the new *dis-* words mean? Ask students to discard the cards with the root words that cannot use *dis-* as a prefix, which provides a physical response to eliminating these words from use with *dis-*. During the week, praise, encourage, and point out students who use *dis-* words in their speaking and writing. Later in the week, as a follow-up activity with students, write out all the *dis-* words students created, one per card. On another set of cards, write the definitions of these words. Can students find the individuals to match the word and the definition?

Finally, there are two cautions about using students' primary language to support the development of morphological knowledge. The first is that *false cognates* are words that look like they might share a similar meaning across languages but actually mean something completely different. For example, *pie* in Spanish means *foot* in English, and *ropa* in Spanish means *clothing* in English. It is always important to seek out which words are true cognates when working across languages. You can find a thorough list of English–Spanish cognates, presented alphabetically, at http:// spanishcognates.org.

The second point is that any language other than English should not be used in the classroom if doing so places any English language learner at an advantage or disadvantage over others. Teachers whose students collectively speak a variety of languages should simultaneously help students develop word consciousness and an appreciation of languages in general, while teaching them to develop and apply morphemic analysis in English. One way of valuing all languages represented in a classroom is to maintain a multilingual word wall with important words, such as essential content words or objects that can be labeled around the classroom.

Developing Spelling Skills

Learning to spell words correctly and read them efficiently greatly assists in automaticity when reading and writing. English language learners should learn to recognize, memorize, and use word patterns without needing to labor over them. This in turn increases their ability to focus on larger "pieces" of language, such as composing an idea and creating meaningful sentences when writing, or reading for comprehension. It frees up working memory to process the use of language for meaning. Only through study, practice, and repeated word pattern manipulation can students accomplish spelling words automatically and efficiently. Again, doing so leads to overall improved use and comprehension of English. This type of learning requires direct and explicit instruction.

The following example presents two lists of words from two different English language learners. Both students are in fourth grade, both are native Spanish speakers, and both wrote a retelling of Steven Kellogg's *Chicken Little* that was read aloud to them. Both were assessed at an intermediate level of English language development on a statewide ELD/ESL assessment test. A close look at their spelling reveals great differences in their literacy abilities and the type of spelling instruction they each need in order to become more fluent at writing and reading.

Can you determine each student's spelling needs by examining the lists of words? Try to establish one strength and two needs for each student. After each word list are observations (strengths), recommendations for instruction, and additional comments.

Student 1	Student 2
ther (there)	one
it (eat)	day
coconat (coconut)	was
skcai, scai (sky)	chicken
laik (like)	walking
foling (falling)	something
bot (but)	hit
thei (they)	sky
av (of)	she
cold (called)	said
sed (said)	coming
dident (didn't)	waht (what)
trox (truck)	the
hem (him)	matter
en (in)	police
ai (I)	
hed (head)	
end (and)	

Student 1 Observations:

This student has stable and consistent sound-symbol ability. She is greatly influenced by Spanish, her primary language, which is a strength in terms of her ability to hear and write down sounds as she hears them (*coconat, sed, foling, cold, trox*).

Student 2 Observations:

This student spells many high-frequency words correctly (*one, she, said, the*) and uses the suffix *-ing* correctly. *Waht* instead of *what* indicates the student knows there is an *h* involved but doesn't quite know where it goes.

Student 1 Recommendations:

- Learn to spell high-frequency words. Here are some examples: *there, but, they, of, said.*

- Take a complete phonics program, focusing especially on vowel sounds—first long vowel sounds, then short vowel sounds.

Student 2 Recommendations:

- Continue to learn high-frequency words.

- Learn Latin and Greek base words and affixes.

- Study homophones (*your/you're, I/eye*).

Student 1 Comments:

English vowel sounds are difficult for Spanish speakers. This student should begin with long vowel sounds because she hears them and uses them in Spanish. She does not use or hear short vowel sounds and patterns after learning long vowel sounds. The only exception is the short *e* sound as in *pet* and *techo* (*roof*). Recall that we cannot learn to spell a sound that we cannot hear and distinguish from others.

This student should practice hearing the differences among short vowel sounds. Blind word sorts would be helpful— sorting pictures of words rather than words based on spelling. Repeated practice will help her begin to discern differences (e.g., *cat*, *cup*, *cot*).

Student 2 Comments:

This student can benefit from studying words from the Academic Word List, as they come up in context in the classroom, especially Latin and Greek base words, and affixes. Recall the teaching vignette above with the cognates *disappear/desaparecer* and *float/flotar*, taken from a read-aloud that the class is listening to. In addition, content words drawn from classroom curriculum is a helpful source from which to draw appropriate spelling words for an English learner at this stage of spelling development.

Authors Donald Bear, Marcia Invernizzi, Shane Templeton, and Francine Johnston in *Words Their Way* (2012), and Lori Helman, Donald Bear, Shane Templeton, Marcia Invernizzi, and Francine Johnston in *Words Their Way with English Learners* (2011), provide an invaluable framework for understanding students' stages of spelling development as well as chapters filled with teaching approaches, ideas, and strategies for each of the levels of spelling development.

Carefully Selecting Vocabulary

Selecting just the right words to teach is no small consideration, given time constraints and the number of words students need to learn.

> "The selection of words for instruction is not a trivial matter ... it is imperative to focus on words children are unlikely to learn on their own through exposure to English oral discourse; it is also important to focus on words children will encounter frequently in text and oral language."
>
> —August, Carlo, Dressler, and Snow (2005, 55)

The authors add that beyond direct instruction and exposure to these words, students must have these words reinforced through games, picture cards, and word wall displays, to mention just a few options.

Many sources state that selecting and studying a small number of wisely-chosen words is more effective than asking students to memorize long lists of words. For example, Kucan (2012) describes her thinking in selecting eight words from a passage for students to learn. Beck, McKeown, and Kucan (2002) provide an example in which ten words are selected for student study. Recall from the opening of this chapter that getting to know too many people at one time is problematic for remembering names, faces, and other important information about them. The same holds true for learning vocabulary words. Do not overload students. It defeats the purpose of exposing them to and teaching them vocabulary.

E. D. Hirsch (2003) offers comments on a chapter written by renowned cognitive psychologist George A. Miller (1969) on our informational processing limits:

> "The second chapter was one of the most famous ones ever written in the field of psychology: 'The Magical Number Seven, Plus or Minus Two: Some Limits on Our Capacity for Processing Information.' The 'magical number seven' turned out to be the approximate number of items ... that you can hold in your conscious mind at one time before they start to evaporate into oblivion. This 'magical number seven' is a limitation that ... afflicts everyone including geniuses."
>
> —Hirsch (2003, 12)

Subsequent research has repeatedly shown this idea to hold true. Selecting seven to nine academic words or head words (see the previous discussion on morphological awareness and cognates), or content-area words, or useful words from read-alouds, or a combination of these of up to seven, eight, or nine is a sufficient number. More than this number of words will cause them to "evaporate into oblivion."

To help teachers guide the careful selection of words, and to consider options beyond the AWL, Beck, McKeown, and Linda Kucan (2008) developed a system that helps teachers sort words into three categories:

- Tier 1 words are frequently used and easily explained (*book, chair, blue*).
- Tier 2 words are most useful to teach (as discussed shortly).
- Tier 3 words are technical words with narrow application in their own fields of study (*protozoa, cosine, secant*).

Criteria for Tier 2 words include the following guidelines:

- explains a concept with a known word
- is a more sophisticated word for one students already know
- is typically not heard in everyday, conversational, non-academic settings

- promotes ongoing classroom instruction

- supports conceptual understanding that students already have

- appears frequently in texts across the curriculum

- builds rich connections to other words and concepts

- in literature, is integral to the plot and/or mood of the story

The following application activity uses the preceding criteria. Which Tier 2 words should a teacher select as essential vocabulary words? Which rationales support the selection of each one? A word list with a brief rationale for each word selection appears in Appendix C.

Fossils are evidence of past life; they are remains or imprints of living things from long ago. They can be leaf prints, shell prints, and skeleton prints. The waste from living things can even become fossils! Different kinds of fossils are created through different processes and different materials. They can be made when a living thing dies and becomes buried by sediments, such as ash from a volcano, mud, sand, or silt. They can be frozen in ice or be mummified when the moisture is sucked up by very low-humidity air. Some fossils have been buried in tar for thousands of years.

Most fossils are made when the soft parts of a living thing decay; the hard parts are turned into something like rock. The minerals of the sediments in which the bodies are buried seep into the hard parts. They become preserved as fossils. In fossils that are made when the whole living thing is frozen or mummified, the soft parts are included, too.

Fossils are more likely to be made when a living thing dies near a body of water than on dry land. Near water, it is likely to be quickly buried. Over thousands of years, the sediments settle into layers that become sedimentary rock. Fossils are often found in sedimentary rock.

(Leveled Texts for Science: Earth and Space Science 2008)

Using Nonlinguistic Representations of Vocabulary

Ensuring multiple modalities for students to process and acquire vocabulary and related concept knowledge is especially important for English language learners. The sections that follow outline several suggestions.

Dramatization and Brief Skits

These can be as simple or involved as the teacher chooses to make them. In Chapter 6, a teaching vignette shows Vance, a fifth-grade teacher, having students act out the concept of taxation without representation after a preview of the important vocabulary. The following teaching vignette has another fifth-grade teacher, Diana, helping students understand *prod* and *wader*, words they have come across in their reading and whose meanings underlie a main point in the text.

> Diana has many English language learners in her fifth-grade classroom. The students have completed reading an article about stingrays. She is reviewing portions of the text and questioning students on their understanding.
>
> "If a stingray sees you coming, is it going to come at you and attack you?" asks Diana.
>
> "Not if you don't bother him," responds Gabriel.
>
> "Right, the fourth line says, 'They will not go out of their way to attack you.' That means they are not going to think, 'I'm going to get him.'" (She uses a pinching hand movement.)
>
> The stingray article points out that when wading, it is wise to be alert and to prod a stingray with a stick to make it move away. To reinforce this point, Diana engages students in a very brief role play of two "waders" and a "stingray." She asks the "stingray" to place himself on the floor to "hide" under the sand.

"OK, Gabriel. You're our wader. Now you're wading in the water. Do one of two things the text tells us. What are you going to do that the passage says? What's the word the text uses?"

Several students in the class respond, "It says prod."

Diana nods and asks, "And what's another word for prod?"

Several students respond, "Poke."

Gabriel "wades" a few steps then he pretends to prod the "stingray" with a stick. The "stingray" scuttles away.

"OK, Susana. You're our next 'wader.' What are you going to do?"

Susana responds, "I'm going to step it."

"Yes, you're going to step on it," says Diana.

Susana "steps" on the "stingray," and it lashes out and stings her.

Diana then asks students to add two new vocabulary words and their definitions to their personal dictionaries.

(Zuñiga-Hill and Yopp 1996)

Note that teachers must be judicious in asking students to act out meanings of words and phrases. The teacher should first consider how the meaning of the text might be demonstrated. If nothing comes to mind, then surely that will also be true for English learners. For example, *elf* and *enchanted* are words that appeared once on an "act it out" list for English learners. Still today, these words are an acting-out puzzle.

Hands-On Material

In the teaching vignette about water tension in the "Building Background Knowledge" section earlier in this chapter, students were introduced to the words *bottle* and *water dropper*. These are simple and unchallenging words, yet they are practical items used in the experiments, and for some students, these were new words. For example, *gotero* is formed from the root word *gota*. In Spanish, *-ero* is an important, productive suffix (e.g., *agujero, basurero, grosero, marinero, paletero*). A student studying affixes in Spanish would surely come across the suffix *-ero*. Although it is an example in Spanish, it underscores the point that teachers have many opportunities to promote word learning and to help students make connections across words and build semantic networks, sometimes in unexpected ways. Never underestimate a chance to help students learn new words and affixes, and make new connections across them.

Tableaux, Timelines, and Process Lines

A *tableau* is an ideal review and vocabulary reinforcement for stories, timelines, and process lines, with a modest amount of text. Let's assume students have heard and read *The Three Little Pigs*. The teacher prepares a condensed story of six, seven, or eight sentences or phrases. The number of sentences depends on students' language level and the learning goals. Here is a possibility:

The first little pig was named Cicero. He loved to play music.

The second little pig was named Hector. He loved to dance and sing.

The third little pig was named Jack. He was a hard worker.

The wolf came along and blew down two houses.

Jack let Cicero and Hector in his house.

They rebuilt the two houses and were happy little pigs.

The sentences are cut up. Small groups of students receive one strip of paper each. The members of each small group read the sentence and figure out how they will reenact it in a "freeze frame." Then, all the small groups together need to figure out the correct order in which to place themselves, according to the story. Once the groups are arranged in the correct order, a member of each tableau or freeze frame can read the assigned sentence. Finally, a narrator can read the script while everyone enjoys the tableaux.

Timelines and process lines follow the same general idea as tableaux but without the enacted freeze frames. What is important is sequence. For example, say students have studied a Disciplinary Core Idea from the Next Generation Science Standards (NGSS 2013) on how food is rearranged in the body to form new energy. The teacher assigns sections of the text for small groups of students to review. Each group selects the key idea or ideas in the assigned section and records it for them. When the groups are done reviewing the text and writing, they need to arrange themselves in the correct order so that the process "occurs in the body" in the correct way. They read aloud what they have written as the important ideas, in order of occurrence. While sequencing expository text, students are not truly making nonlinguistic representations. However, the strategy does give students the chance to review text, garner and write down main ideas (that link reading, writing, and speaking), and move around the room as a physical response to the information they are learning.

Vocabulary Self-Selection Strategy (VSS)

The nonlinguistic aspect of this strategy is that one of the four elements of describing the vocabulary item is the student's own nonlinguistic depiction of what the word means. In this process, the student or small group reads the same piece of text. The student selects a word that he or she does not know and believes is either interesting or important enough to the text to share with others. Folding a sheet of paper in fourths, the student writes the word in the upper-left quadrant, and in the upper-right quadrant, the student writes the sentence in which the word was found. Each student orally shares the word, and everyone makes guesses at what each word means. Each student then finds the definition of the selected word and writes it in the lower-left quadrant. In the lower-right quadrant, the student draws a picture that somehow describes the word or the intent of the word. In addition to forming nonlinguistic representations, students are actively engaging with specific vocabulary words that, in a sense, they have selected to "own." Further, this strategy provides multiple exposures to the word (see the next section).

Using Repetition and Multiple Exposures

As stated in the opening of this chapter, getting to know a person requires many encounters and experiences with the individual in various contexts in order to find out who he or she really is. This means building a relationship over time with that person and learning how he or she interacts with others. These ideas exactly mirror vocabulary development. Students need a minimum of ten exposures to a word to begin to

- understand the word and how it is related to other words;
- learn in which contexts to use it correctly;
- learn its synonyms and antonyms; and
- understand and use its shades of meaning.

Knowing a word is a question of degree. This vocabulary learning process has been referred to as developing *depth of meaning* (Graves 1987). Here is just one example: in the previous teaching vignette about the stingray, a student answered, "I'm going to step it." Right meaning and use, but it needs the word *on*.

However, consider other common uses of *step*:

- step up
- Step it up!
- step in the right direction
- in step with
- step into
- Step on it!
- step over
- step-by-step
- Watch your step!

The list goes on. Yes, it is true that knowing a word and using it well is a question of degree and involves developing a depth of meaning in order to use it correctly. The following sections present some strategies that provide repeated, multiple exposures to vocabulary.

Chants, Rhymes, and Songs

Chants, rhymes, and songs have a way of embedding themselves in our minds and are therefore excellent reinforcement and repetition of the words that go along with them. Another GLAD strategy (Brechtel 2001), in addition to the pictorial input chart (see Chapter 5), offers the "Farmer in the Dell" chant as a way to reinforce vocabulary as well as to learn parts of grammar. Let's assume students are studying Disciplinary Core Idea ESS.1.C, History of Planet Earth (NGSS 2013).

After each lesson in the unit, the teacher asks students to collectively complete a chart with the words they have found during each lesson that fit the grammatical categories shown in Figure 5.4. Teacher modeling and assistance are needed until students catch on to the categories. In addition to reinforcing content-area words, the chart helps students become more aware of grammatical categories.

Figure 5.4 Planet Earth Chant

Article	Adjective	Noun	Verb	Adverb	Prepositional Phrase
the	explosive	fossils	seeps	clearly	into the sea
an	giant	volcano	erupts	quickly	inside caves
a	hard	plates (tectonic)	flows	slowly	over time
	melted	core	drifts		over the Earth
	glowing	mantel	shifts		under the sea
	heavy	crust	scrapes		next to rivers
	huge	lava	slides		
		landmass	grates		

Then, when sufficient numbers of words are collected, students create and sing meaningful and content-correct sentences by selecting one word from each category, placing the words together, and singing them to the tune of "The Farmer in the Dell." Here are three examples:

The explosive, glowing lava,

The explosive, glowing lava,

The explosive, glowing lava erupts quickly into the sea.

The giant, heavy fossils,

The giant, heavy fossils,

The giant, heavy fossils form slowly next to rivers.

The hard, heavy plates,

The hard, heavy plates,

The hard, heavy plates drift slowly over the Earth.

Teachers can use their imaginations and knowledge of songs to explore other singing possibilities. Another option is the call and response military cadence "I don't know but I've been told …"

I don't know but I've been told

Cleopatra's crown was jewels and gold.

I don't know but Egyptian trade

Started getting them all the money they made.

Found Poetry

This GLAD strategy makes an excellent unit review. Making a found poem may take two or three lessons to complete. The teacher provides a piece of informational text on a familiar topic that includes vocabulary students have studied. Students read it and highlight words that they particularly notice or are drawn to, or that they know. The teacher (or students) writes these words and phrases on sentence strips. Students decide how to arrange these strips in a pocket chart (or on a table surface) in a way that sounds pleasing to them. Phrases can be cut up and words can be rearranged but not used more than one time, except for the title. The teacher can provide small groups with the same vocabulary and phrases, and then ask each group to create its own poem.

Semantic Feature Analysis (SFA)

As with found poetry, SFA is an excellent review tool. A teacher can also use it while working through a unit of study to help students clarify understanding of important vocabulary. The first step is for the teacher to select the important vocabulary words and decide on qualities or characteristics they may or may not share. The teacher then creates a grid with vocabulary words along the side and qualities or characteristics along the top. The teacher and students together decide which features are true or false, and indicate this with a plus sign (+) or a minus (−) sign, discussing and focusing on the vocabulary items. Figure 5.5 shows an example from a unit about pets. Figure 5.6 shows an example from a piece of literature. Figure 5.7 shows an example that compares longstanding civilizations.

Figure 5.5 My Favorite Pet

	has fur or hair	has babies live	is warm blooded	is cold blooded	has scales	has four feet	eats only meat (carnivorous)	eats everything (omnivorous)
snake								
goat								
cat								
hamster								
lizard								
parakeet								
dog								
turtle								

Figure 5.6 Characters' Demonstrated Qualities

	gained independence	overcame fear	showed wisdom	found solutions to problems
Justine				
Diego				
Mamá				
Alfredo				

Figure 5.7 The World's Great Civilizations

	relied on agriculture	depended on trade	maintained an army	was monotheistic
Byzantine				
Egyptian				
Greek				
Ottoman				

In addition to offering multiple exposures to vocabulary and deepening understanding, SFA is beneficial because it

- provides opportunities for students to discuss and apply the many academic verbs used in the CCSS, requiring students to compare and contrast, identify, justify, support, and so on;

- requires focused and academic student discussion, another aspect emphasized in the CCSS Speaking and Listening Standards;

- helps clarify the relationships among concepts or entities being compared; and

- can be used as an assessment tool to check for understanding.

Wordless Picture Books

In addition to providing excellent structures for writing (discussed more fully in Chapter 7), wordless picture books offer opportunities for repeated exposure to and use of vocabulary. A wordless picture book uses the same characters and many of the same objects throughout the book. This provides opportunities for exposure to the same vocabulary and writing opportunities for students' own storytelling using this repeated vocabulary.

The following wordless picture books lend themselves well to oral storytelling with opportunities for practicing focused vocabulary:

- *Hug* by Jez Alborough

- *The Snowman* by Raymond Briggs

- *Good Dog, Carl* by Alexandra Day

- *Wave* by Suzy Lee
- *The Lion and the Mouse* by Jerry Pinkney
- *A Boy, a Dog, and a Frog* by Mercer Mayer
- *Pancakes for Breakfast* by Tomie dePaola

Teaching Students Strategies to Help Themselves

One of a teacher's primary goals is to instruct students on how to become independent learners and thinkers. The following sections outline strategies that promote independent word study.

Morphological Analysis

This strategy, discussed previously in the section "Morphological Awareness, Cognates, and the Need for Direct Instruction," is a powerful tool for students to learn to use on their own. Children begin acquiring a sense of meaning-carrying morphemes at a very young age (Yopp, Yopp, and Bishop 2009). Examples are *look, see, go,* and *sit.* Young English-speaking children sometimes use the morpheme *-ed* inappropriately, such as *go-ed* (meaning *went*), *sitted* (meaning *sat*), and *see-d* (meaning *saw*). This is because at a young age they have already learned that *-ed* is a morpheme used to indicate past tense, and they apply it to all verbs. They have not yet learned the correct forms of these irregular verbs. English learners need to have these meaning-carrying morphemes pointed out to them as soon as possible for two important reasons:

- The ability to break down words when encountering them is a powerful vocabulary development tool. A substantial amount of research shows that helping students develop and learn to apply English language morphological awareness provides "multiple important roles in English reading comprehension for students from a variety of home language backgrounds" (Kieffer and Lesaux 2012, 1170), as pointed out in the discussion in the section "Morphological Awareness, Cognates, and the Need for Direct Instruction."

- As early as first grade, the Common Core State Standards expects students to identify common root words (*look, use*) and by third grade know and use common affixes and root words.

Word Clouds, Word Sifts, and Visual Dictionaries

These are powerful online sources for digitally displaying frequently used words in texts supported by an immense amount of related information with just a few clicks. One such resource to consider looking at before reading further is WordSift (http://www.wordsift.com/site/about).

Here are just a few examples of the potential of WordSift. The teacher or student can copy and paste a piece of text into the appropriate text box. The first image that appears is the fifty most frequently used words in that text, with the frequency of words indicated by font size. The most common word appears in the largest font.

Another option is to click any of the words, which takes the user to the relevant word web. It is possible to select words in the text that are common across the discipline. Another possibility is to go to the related Academic Word List (AWL) and look at the related words in the text that have different meanings across disciplines—for example, *tension* carries a different meaning in science than in social science. These are just some examples of the possibilities available.

An example of a visual dictionary with multiple nodes that link a single word to related verbs, adjectives, synonyms, antonyms, and more, in a visually playful and appealing way, is Visuwords™ (http://www.visuwords.com).

Word clouds, word sifts, and visual dictionaries promote engaged and proactive learning, encourage individual and small-group learning, and are broadly adaptable. Not only are these resources student self-help tools, but they are also powerful means through which teachers can promote learning in a multitude of ways, connecting students to technology in the classroom in ways that they are becoming increasingly accustomed to in all aspects of their lives.

Using Read-Alouds

A critical aspect of the curriculum for English learners is reading aloud from all genres: biographies, essays, stories, informational books, and poetry. There are several reasons for this:

- **Read-alouds introduce students to new words and concepts** that are beyond their own reading level. They provide ways to share information that students would be unable to read on their own (Biemiller 2003; Helman et al. 2011).

- **Read-alouds provide background knowledge** and broad contexts in which to understand new vocabulary.

- **Read-alouds allow for discussion and clarification** of new words and concepts.

- **Informational read-alouds are excellent for making connections** with units of study, therefore broadening students' understanding and related vocabulary (Helman et al. 2011). Hearing vocabulary repeated and used in different contexts deepens students' understanding and ability to use these words.

- **Read-alouds introduce new words and concepts** that are not used in everyday conversation, and they permit students to hear these new words in the context of written language.

- **Repeated read-alouds permit students to hear, process, and understand** increasingly larger pieces of language (Goldenberg 2008).

- **Read-alouds provide English learners with opportunities to hear the natural cadences and rhythms of English** (Peregoy and Boyle 2013). Hearing the natural stress, pitch, and intonation patterns is an important aspect of learning a new language.

Poetry is an excellent read-aloud source for hearing various rhymes and rhythms of English. Works by the following long-beloved poets are good starting places:

- Dr. Seuss

- Jack Prelutsky

- Shel Silverstein

The following websites contain a wealth of excellent children's poetry:

- **Children's poet laureate Kenn Nesbitt's** site (htpp://www.poetry4kids.com) features poetry as well as other resources ranging from podcasts, to contests, to instruction for students about writing their own poetry.

- **The Poetry Foundation** website (htpp://www.poetryfoundation.org) includes an array of resources such as featured poets, poems categorized by themes and by poets, and poets reading their own works. It is important for English language learners to hear other adult voices in addition to their teacher's voice modeling good English.

- **PoemHunter.com** (http://www.poemhunter.com/poems/children/) is a rich resource that includes a list of the top 500 poems, a poem of the day, poems about topics listed alphabetically, and more.

Shorter selections for beginning English learners are appropriate. This is because listening and trying to understand stretches of oral language can be tiring, especially in the beginning stages of language learning. In addition to the comprehension level and length of a piece, students' interests should be considered. Brief previews of the title, main idea, and important vocabulary with "showing" explanations are very helpful.

Applying Narrow Reading

It is widely recognized that wide reading is an excellent way to expand vocabulary. However, for English language learners, there are compelling reasons to promote what Stephen Krashen calls narrow reading (2004). Narrow reading, or reading deeply on the same topic that uses the same or similar vocabulary and concepts, provides multiple opportunities to process and learn words (see the section "Using Repetition and Multiple Exposures"). Books on the same or similar topics, series books, and books by the same author are examples of narrow reading. This concept applies to both informational text and fiction. Narrow reading is effective for the following reasons:

- A student can develop vocabulary and concepts by focusing on just one topic or concentrated reading area (Hadaway 2009).

- Each topic has its own vocabulary, so narrow reading helps the student build a network of relationships between known words and new ones (Hadaway 2009).

- Repeated exposure to similar vocabulary in a variety of text exposes the student to increasingly richer ways of understanding and using that vocabulary (Yopp, Yopp, and Bishop 2009).

- Repeated exposure to related vocabulary and concepts develops a schema for the topic and builds background knowledge for further understanding.

Text sets, books that address the same or related topic, are a way to implement narrow reading. Stair-step text sets refers to arranging text sets from easier to increasingly more difficult reading levels (Hadaway 2009), another way to support English language learners. Thematic instruction should include stair-step text sets so that students can read information at varying levels of sophistication on the same topic.

The following list is just one example of a text set of easy to mid-level readers and resources for students who are fascinated by spiders. Alternatively, these sources could support activities developed for a learning center.

- *National Geographic Readers: Spiders* by Laura Marsh
- *Hidden Spiders* by Simon Pollard
- *Spiders* by Nic Bishop
- *Spider's Lunch: All About Garden Spiders* by Joanna Cole
- *Spiders* by Gail Gibbons
- *Spiders* by Andrew Miller

Two more online sources for intermediate to advanced level English learners are as follows:

- KidZone's spider page: http://www.kidzone.ws/lw/spiders/index.htm
- K–3 Learning Pages, listserv/web resources related to spiders: http://www.k-3learningpages.net/web%20spiders.htm

Using *All About …* books by author Jim Arnosky is another way to implement narrow reading in the classroom. These books about animals use the same physical layout and text structure and include basic information on each animal's habitat and activities. Similarly, informational books by author Gail Gibbons offer readers a consistent format and information with approachable vocabulary and concepts.

Consider narrow reading with fiction books, as fully discussed in Chapter 6. Series books use similar vocabulary and story structures or formats. The main characters maintain the same traits and characteristics, and they typically use certain words and speak in particular ways. The stories take place in the same or a similar environment. Furthermore, a reader can pick up on the rhythm of the author's style and the text organization (Hadaway 2009). These elements lead to a repetition of vocabulary and provide overall comprehension scaffolding or, as Krashen states, comprehensible context (Krashen 2004).

For English language learners, narrow reading is a highly supportive approach. It offers more exposure to specific vocabulary and makes for a deeper understanding of new vocabulary. It permits students to see increasingly familiar vocabulary and concepts in a variety of texts so that they can begin to own these words and concepts and use them in their daily life when speaking and writing.

As with the previous teaching vignette on water tension, the following lesson was taught to teacher credential candidates who were enrolled in a language arts methods course (in the United States). Here, they experience a "shoe on the other foot" lesson in Portuguese.

The students had completed two university class sessions (about six hours) on promoting vocabulary development with elementary-level students.

They were introduced to a children's story in Portuguese, appropriate for primary students titled *A velha árvore (The Old Tree)* by Ruth Hürlmann.

- They were introduced to nine important words and their meanings.

- The story was read to them. They followed along in their own copies of the story.

- They had opportunities to match individual pictures with definitions and then match the pictures and definitions to those that appeared in the book.

After the lesson, they were asked which strategies they used to help them understand the story. Here is how they responded:

- nonlinguistic representations

- slowly spoken language from the teacher

- teacher's emphasis on important words

- a great deal of repetition and multiple exposures

- analyzing word parts

- looking for cognates

- visual context clues (pictures)

- physical manipulation of photocopied pictures from the story

- matching pictures and words

- active engagement in manipulating pictures and definitions

- added wait time

- explicit, front-loaded vocabulary in advance of the story

- multiple modalities in using the vocabulary

- hearing words in context

Their responses show that they used many of the same strategies discussed throughout this chapter. Personal experiences such as these often help teachers remember to use strategies and approaches that help English language learners develop new vocabulary and improve understanding.

Summary

As with people, words surround us every day and significantly impact us. How we use words and how other people use words underpin all communication. Therefore, learning words and learning to use them well is essential. The following aspects of vocabulary development should be intentionally planned for and embedded across every aspect of the curriculum:

- high-frequency words

- spelling patterns

- morphemic analysis, noting that the Common Core promote learning of root words and suffixes from the first grade

- high quality of a small number of carefully selected content words used across the curriculum

- opportunities for repeated exposure to words that have been taught and studied

- indirect exposure to rich vocabulary, such as through read-alouds and independent reading

- curiosity about words

- instruction that promotes ways to teach students independence in learning new vocabulary

- listening, speaking, reading, and writing opportunities with focused vocabulary woven throughout them every school day

Students should be encouraged and supported in using new vocabulary in speaking and writing. After all, the goal of learning new vocabulary is ultimately using it correctly and enhancing communication. Only then can we say we truly know a word.

Apply, Reflect, and Extend

1. Which of the nine key topics discussed in this chapter do you most want to incorporate into your teaching? How do you plan to do this?

2. What have been your experiences learning vocabulary in English or in another language? Given what you have read in this chapter, what was done well and what was missing from the experience?

3. In the context of what you have read about in this chapter, what are strengths of your vocabulary instruction? What would you most like to improve? How has what you have read been helpful?

4. Which strategy would be most helpful for beginning English learners? For advanced English learners?

5. Design a lesson using the preview strategy.

6. Design a semantic feature analysis chart that relates to a current or upcoming unit.

Chapter 6

Helping English Learners Who Are Reading to Learn

Anticipatory Quiz

Are the following statements true or false?

_____ **1.** Broad constructs have little practical classroom application in helping teachers of English language learners.

_____ **2.** Beyond using visuals and realia, limited approaches exist for helping English learners grasp abstract concepts.

_____ **3.** Overall text structures are useful patterns for English learners to pay attention to.

_____ **4.** Fixed group membership in cooperative learning groups provides needed structure for English learners.

_____ **5.** Primary language support should be limited.

_____ **6.** Reading comprehension strategies such as monitoring and summarizing can be effectively used with English learners.

In the third grade, students begin the curve toward reading increasingly challenging material to learn subject-matter content. English learners are particularly taxed in learning to read for meaning, or reading to learn. This chapter addresses eight key constructs that are essential background knowledge for teachers of English learners. They help teachers consider and make instructional decisions to benefit their students. The eight constructs are as follows:

- Place instruction on the concrete-to-abstract continuum.

- Make meaning visible.

- Point out and teach patterns and structures.

- Talk first, read later.

- Provide multiple passes and processes.

- Seek and use primary language support.

- Provide structured interactive learning opportunities.

- Use direct-instruction strategies to promote reading comprehension.

You might think of these constructs as the plain white walls of a living room: no one especially notices them—unless they are not there. Or you might think of them as "the little voice in your head" when it comes to planning and teaching: *How* am I making abstract concepts visible and comprehensible? *How* am I helping students see patterns and structures? *How* am I using multiple passes and processes? Teaching vignettes and strategies are embedded throughout this chapter to illustrate ways that the eight constructs work in the classroom with students.

Place Instruction on the Concrete-to-Abstract Continuum

Teacher A is planning a unit on the history of planet Earth (NGSS 2013). The key concepts are as follows:

- The examination rock strata and fossils provides helpful clues to understand Earth's history.

- Results of earthquakes, mountains, and volcanoes provide data that can be studied and reveals a great deal of information.

- Examination and analysis use graph and chart data.

- Slow and large geological processes, such as slow plate motion, affect Earth's surface.

- Small and rapid events, such as landslides and geothermal reactions, affect Earth's surface.

Teacher B is planning a unit on ancient Egypt. The key concepts are as follows:

- The Nile River served as a vital resource that supported transportation and agricultural development.

- The ancient Egyptians built an economic surplus based on the Nile River's resources.

- Economic strength contributed to Egypt's political and cultural power.

- The ancient Egyptians developed a complex society of social classes, roles, and responsibilities.

- Rulers extended ancient Egypt's trade, wealth, and power.

- The Egyptians made many advances in geometry, medicine, agriculture, and astronomy.

- The Egyptians developed many systems: a writing system, a counting system, a linear measuring system, systems to measure time, and a religious structure.

- Ancient Egypt was a strong and unified civilization that maintained religious, social, and political order for nearly 3,000 years.

Two important aspects in the planning process are each teacher's background knowledge and whether or not the teacher has previously taught the unit. For teachers of English learners, a third very important aspect is how concrete or how abstract the concepts are. Concrete, context-embedded concepts, such as "The examination of rock strata and fossils provides helpful clues to understand Earth's history" can be demonstrated in tangible ways. Abstract ideas such as "Ancient Egyptians built an economic surplus based on the Nile River's resources" can be challenging to demonstrate in tangible ways. Concrete ideas are relatively language independent—that is, they can be demonstrated and shown without having to depend on a great amount of language to explain them. Conversely, abstract ideas are very language dependent. They rely almost exclusively on language to explain; therefore, they are more challenging to make tangible and comprehensible.

If asked to place each unit of study along the concrete-to-abstract continuum, most teachers would place the Earth science unit toward the concrete end of the continuum and the ancient Egypt unit at the abstract end of the continuum, as shown in Figure 6.1.

Figure 6.1 Example Units on a Concrete-to-Abstract Continuum

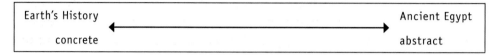

Many important ideas in the Earth history unit can be conveyed in a "let me show you" manner that promotes understanding. Teachers have several possible ways to go about showing students meaning and engaging them in understanding. For example, students can examine fossils and photos of rock strata. They can be shown what happens when tectonic plates move, examine diagrams of Earth's layers or the structure of a volcano, and observe and participate in a simulated earthquake experiment. Teachers can then tie language back into these "showing" experiences to promote concept and vocabulary development.

Conversely, most teachers would place the ancient Egypt unit at the abstract end of the continuum because ideas such as the following are challenging to make concrete without trivializing them:

- Ancient Egyptians built an economic surplus based on the Nile River's resources.

- Egypt was a strong and unified civilization that maintained religious, social, and political order for nearly 3,000 years.

Making an abstract concept comprehensible requires careful and creative planning. Abstract ideas take time to develop, explain, and for students to process, so they require small steps through several lessons approached in the most concrete ways possible. In this case, showing pictures and giving brief descriptions of Egyptian farmers, miners, hunters, and sailors who navigated the Nile River would be a starting point. This could be followed by demonstrating how the work of ancient Egyptians produced important products and money. A subsequent lesson could demonstrate how bartering occurred, which in turn created wealth. Another lesson may require students to categorize the types of work people in ancient Egypt did and their relative social relationships. Collectively, these concrete lessons contribute to the ideas that ancient Egypt was a wealthy nation; ancient Egypt's people had various roles and responsibilities, with some providing labor and others ruling over political and religious structures.

It is essential for a teacher of English learners to give careful thought to how concrete or abstract any unit and lesson will be. This decision will determine the kind of teaching required. That is, how language-independent (concrete) or how language-dependent (abstract) will instruction need to be. The more concrete and language-independent the instruction, as in the Earth unit, the more comprehensible and accessible the information can be made for students. On the other hand, language-dependent (abstract) concepts that rely a great deal on language to explain meanings, like the important ideas about ancient Egypt, will be more challenging for English learners to understand. The effective teacher finds ways to create small steps with concrete examples in building comprehension of abstract ideas.

Making Decisions About Concrete-to-Abstract Instruction

Here is an opportunity to think about teaching in terms of the concrete-to-abstract continuum. Place the name of the unit of study along the continuum below. Briefly explain your reasoning. The answers and explanations appear in Appendix C.

1. Weather and climate: Scientists record data to compare patterns and make predictions

2. A literature study of *Sarah, Plain and Tall*

3. The ancient Roman Empire: Causes and effects of the expansion and disintegration of the Roman Empire

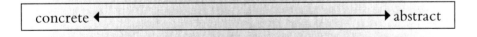

concrete ←——————————————————→ abstract

A teaching vignette in the following "Make Meaning Visible" section demonstrates how Vance, a fifth grade teacher, provided concrete ways for his students to build an understanding of the abstract idea that taxation without representation was an important contributing factor to the American Revolution.

Make Meaning Visible

The important idea of making meaning visible is to "show, not tell," just as a good writer does. It means unpacking meaning and clearly laying it out for inspection and understanding. As discussed in the previous section, the more abstract concepts and vocabulary are, the more important it is for effective teachers to find ways to make meaning visible. Imagine a suitcase whose contents are unknown. While it is possible to make random guesses about what the suitcase contains, it is much more effective to unpack the suitcase and lay out the contents piece by piece to make the content visible. This is what English language learners need: they need information to be unpacked. They need to be able to "see" it and even to touch it to comprehend. Approaches that can show and explain meaning such as timelines, concept maps, short dramas and play acting, tactile objects, and graphic organizers that exhibit limited amounts of text to show relationships among ideas are all very helpful. James Cummins puts it this way: "Language and content will be acquired most successfully when students are challenged cognitively but provided with the contextual and linguistic supports or scaffolds for successful task completion" (2000, 71).

The following teaching vignette demonstrates how Vance worked with his fifth-grade English learners to help them understand one of the key causes of the American Revolution: taxation without representation. Notice that he also uses the construct of "talk first, read later," which is described later in the chapter.

> In planning for the unit of study on the American Revolution, Vance decided he wanted all of his students to understand that one of its main causes was that of taxation without representation. After viewing an introductory video and completing a whole class KWL (know-want-learn) chart, Vance gathered the English learners for a preview lesson prior to reading the social studies textbook material. The English-only and advanced English learners were completing an "into" anticipatory activity in small groups.

Vance asked the English learners to write down the words *taxes*, *represent*, and *representation* in their social studies journals. Then he said, "Look, here's a newspaper ad for a pair of athletic shoes on sale for $35.99. Is that exactly what you pay—$35.99?" The students say that they would have to pay more—"Extra money," says one student. Vance nods and says, "This extra money is the tax on the shoes. It goes to the government. Taxes pay for schools, to fix the streets, to build parks, and other things for us." He draws pictures as he talks to explain: a school building, a street, a park, and dollar signs.

Then Vance asks the students who they elected from the class to go to student council. "Edwin," they say. "Yes, Edwin represents all of us: Room 7. He says what we want and what we don't want. He shares our ideas. He talks for us." Some of the students nod.

"Now we're going to do a little play with the words *taxes* and *represent*," says Vance. He moves the students around. "Jorge, you're the king of England. You sit on this special chair—your throne. Thaís, you're a colonist working in your store. You're selling things. Noé, you're a colonist working hard on your farm. You are working. Antonio, you are the king's representative— like Edwin is our representative. Now, the king tells Antonio to get money. You go get money—taxes—from the colonists."

Antonio walks from Jorge, "the king," over to the colonists and puts his hands out as if to receive money.

Vance tells the students to hold their poses while he shows them illustrations from the social studies book. "England needs the money. They had a big war with France for seven years. The war cost England lots of money. And now they need money— taxes from the colonists. They have to pay for the war. Colonists, do you like this? Do you want to give your money to Antonio for the king and for the government in England? Do you want to pay taxes?"

Noé bursts out, "The king—and the government in England—they tell the colonists they have to pay the money—eh—the taxes—but the colonists—we say *no!* We didn't tell you we gonna pay! We no gonna pay you nothing! Go home. We don't get a … a … represent …"

"Yes," says Vance. "This is exactly the idea. The colonists did not think this is fair. The colonists did not agree to pay extra taxes. They did not want to pay taxes to England. The government in England did not ask them. They just made the colonists pay without talking about it with them. This is taxation without representation. Now you can write this important idea in your journals. *The colonists did not want to pay taxes to England. It was taxation without representation.*"

For his lesson, Vance identified an important abstract, language-dependent idea. Then, he created incremental steps that built meaning in a concrete way to help his students understand it.

Point Out and Teach Patterns and Structures

In discussing elements of language, Chapter 2 highlights the importance of language patterns. These can be found at all levels of language: in sound patterns, written spelling patterns, grammatical patterns, or structures that support large pieces of text. Discerning patterns and structures is a critical component of language learning, whether a first or second language, whether oral or written language, and whether within-word language patterns or text structures.

As children learn to read, they notice small and then increasingly larger patterns in written language, and they rely on available clues. The following is an example.

Fabian, an early reader, recognizes *M, m, i,* and *Mi,* and he knows that Mickey (Mouse) begins with *Mi.* At this early point in his reading, he "reads" any word beginning with *Mi* as Mickey, whether the word is Mike or Mitch or another name or noun that appears at the beginning of a sentence and therefore starts with *Mi.*

Printed with permission from Fabian Guanio

Second language readers begin to process text in the same way, looking for familiar patterns, whether within-word patterns as just shown or larger patterns as will be discussed next.

Here is an example of another type of pattern: a whole piece or "chunk" of a verbal pattern learned by a second language learner.

An English-speaking teacher was learning Spanish phrases to use on occasion with her students. She would say to them at the end of the school day, "*Adios, estudiantes. Hasta mañana.*" Her students would sometimes respond with the phrase "*Sí maestra. Si Dios quiere.*"

One day when her students said "*Adios, maestra,*" she responded with "*Si Dios quiere,*" not really understanding what it meant but knowing that it was appropriate in that context. The students began laughing and cheering her on. Puzzled and a bit worried, she asked them what she had said that was so funny. What does "*Si Dios quiere*" mean? They told her that it's an expression in response to a leave-taking meaning "the Good Lord willing." They laughed approvingly because she had learned yet another phrase and had begun to use it appropriately.

This oral-language pattern that the teacher learned is similar to the way that a young preliterate child who is read stories learns to use "once upon a time" and "the end." It is a whole piece of learned language, complete with appropriate prosody (stress, pitch, and intonation) that fits into a particular context. It is important for English learners to be frequently exposed to natural language patterns and usage because they are another way of learning aspects of English.

A proficient reader does not take in every syllable; rather, he or she relies on language patterns and other clues to make sense of written language. When reading in an unfamiliar language, these patterns become even more important. To provide a sense of the importance of written patterns, what follows is a sentence written in Portuguese and what a Portuguese learner could deduce from it, using his background knowledge (computers, software, English, and Spanish) and knowledge of a grammatical language pattern that indicates a series of things, as in A, B, and C.

"... *a maioria dos softwares gratuitos são baixados da Internet, não apenas em smartphones, mas também para uso em computadores pessoais e laptops.*"

Using the pattern, ____ , ____ , and ____ , he deduced that one of the words he didn't know (*pessoais*) was desktops or PCs. So he deduced that the phrase was something like "smartphones, ____ , computers, and laptops."

The reader understood the whole sentence to be something close to "You can get software from the Internet for smartphones, (something), computers, and laptops."

The translated sentence is "... the majority of free software is downloaded from the Internet, not just on smartphones, but also for use on personal computers and laptops."

Printed with permission from Burnie Dunlap

It is helpful for teachers to point out grammatical patterns to students. English language learners are well served by learning to pay attention to them in processing text.

Because high interest, low reading level (hi-lo) books adhere to the most common English sentence pattern of subject-predicate (e.g., "The dog ran quickly up the sidewalk"), they are ideal for English learners. Hi-lo books' straightforward sentence structure helps for three reasons. First, this sentence pattern mirrors the most common structure students hear. Second, it reinforces this standard English pattern and serves as a model for speaking and writing. Third, because it is the pattern students hear, know, and expect, the pattern fits their sentence schema and makes the text easier to process. For additional support, hi-lo texts include clearly explained and simplified vocabulary used repeatedly to reinforce meaning and clear illustrations to further support the text's meaning. The following are two examples from a hi-lo text on Earth and space science. They illustrate the use of the basic English sentence pattern (subject-predicate) and use clearly explained and repeated vocabulary.

Think of Earth as a hard-boiled egg. An egg has a shell. Earth has a crust. An egg has liquid under its shell. Earth has hot magma under its crust. The Earth is much bigger than an egg. It is 6,400 kilometers (4,000 miles) from its crust down to its center!

(*Leveled Texts for Science: Earth and Space Science* 2008)

A volcano spits out melted rock, or magma. Magma comes from deep in the Earth. It pushes through where there is a weak spot in the crust. Most volcanoes happen near the edge of Earth's plates. The stress at the edges makes the crust weak. This lets magma burst out.

(*Leveled Texts for Science: Earth and Space Science* 2008)

As noted earlier, patterns or structures exist at every level of text and assist in the language learning process. For intermediate to early-advanced English learners, series books provide very helpful overall structures. That is, the reader knows that the main character behaves in a certain way, has similar types of problems to solve or overcome, typically uses certain words or speaks in a particular way, and interacts with others in a certain way, and the story will take place in the same or a similar environment. The following is an interview with a student who reads every one of author Jeff Kinney's *Wimpy Kid* books he can find.

C: Why do you like to read *Wimpy Kid* books?

J: 'Cause Greg—he gets in trouble. He has a lot of problems and he get in trouble. He's weak … he … he doesn't work out. He plays video games a lot.

C: What about his brother Roderick? Do they get along? Do they like each other?

J: No. They fight a lot. Roderick he's kind of dumb. He's dirty… he disgusts.

C: He's disgusting?

J: Yeah, disgusting.

C: Do you learn any words when you read *Wimpy Kid* books?

J: Yeah.

C: Can you think of any?

J: Like *insurance* and *snow days*.

C: Do you look at the pictures? The drawings?

J: Yeah, sometimes. You can see Greg all weak and skinny.

Printed with permission from Julius Guanio

From this interview, it is evident that the overall text structures the student expects are as follows: problems and trouble for Greg, who is a weakling and who fights with his brother Roderick, who Greg believes is disgusting. The student may not understand every word of the story, although he is reading it, enjoying it, and is beginning to make sense of text and story through the use of the overall patterns. Stephen Krashen (2004) calls this narrow reading, highlighting the importance of this approach for English language learners (also discussed in Chapters 4 and 5). In his article, Krashen uses the example of a high school English language learner who became enthralled with Francine Pascal's *Sweet Valley High* books. Just as with the student in the preceding interview, the high school English learner came to rely on familiar story structures: the same settings, the same characters and how they interacted, the characters' problems and dilemmas, and the common vocabulary used throughout the series. Reading this series helped her learn English.

It is important to help English learners seek patterns and structures when they are reading. The usefulness of particular patterns or structures depends on two aspects: the stage of English language development of the student and the student's age. For example, is the student a kindergartner or first grader at the beginning stage? Then, hearing and seeing short patterns in text are important to point out to the student. Intermediate English learners in mid-to-upper grades will be well served by series stories with the same characters and story structure. The following is a list of popular series books that can be fun and useful for English learners. These series books provide more concrete situations (less fantasy based, less science fiction) and are therefore more readily understood reading experiences.

- *Arthur* by Marc Brown
- *Big Nate* by Lincoln Peirce
- *Captain Underpants* by Dav Pilkey
- *Clifford the Big Red Dog* by Norman Bridwell
- *Diary of a Wimpy Kid* by Jeff Kinney
- *How I Survived Middle School* by Nancy E. Krulik
- *Middle School* by James Patterson
- *Curious George* by H. A. Rey and Margaret Rey
- *Dear Dumb Diary* by Jim Benton
- *Dork Diaries* by Rachel Renée Russell

Talk First, Read Later

Oral language ability is a key factor for successful English learners. It is also an aspect of instruction that can receive a quick and insufficient pass. A student needs to listen to and speak about new ideas and new vocabulary prior to being able to read and understand them. Not only does talking first and reading later help English learners develop conceptual knowledge and vocabulary prior to processing a piece of text, but it also helps them practice and develop important speaking and listening skills.

Recall that English learners often have a double cognitive load of simultaneously learning English while learning in English. Through hearing and speaking about important concepts and vocabulary before reading about them, English learners are building their knowledge and understanding, and therefore building their ability to read with more comprehension than if they had had no prior exposure and discussion. Front-loading as a teaching strategy is very successful with English learners. It refers to the practice of previewing information prior to the lesson or unit, thereby providing a jump-start on hearing and grasping understanding of these words and phrases.

The following teaching vignette features a fifth-grade teacher who used a great deal of up-front class discussion followed by reading the social studies text later. It is evident that although the English speaker who posed the question in this vignette was very limited in his ability to produce language, he clearly had a good understanding of the concepts involved—enough to "ask" a one-word question for the "Want to Know" column of the KWL chart the class was constructing.

Diana's students were engaged in a KWL activity on the Westward Movement. The students were adding what they knew about a topic, and what they wanted to know. Various students contributed to the "know" and "want to know" sections of the large chart taped along the length of the blackboard. Within the context of questions about covered wagons, an English learner raised his hand. Diana called on him and he simply said "Why...?" as he moved his hand in a choppy circle. Diana says, "Oh! Why did the wagons form a circle at night?" The student smiles and nods as Diana wrote the question on the chart. "Good question," added Diana.

(Zuñiga-Hill and Yopp 1996)

Although at an early stage of English development, the student was able to express a nearly wordless question, reflecting his engagement in the class discussion. Diana accepted the student's intended meaning, complimented him for his contribution, and provided a verbal and written model for expressing his intended meaning.

Investing in discussion prior to reading is time very well spent. In the preceding teaching vignette, the teacher had invested two social studies class periods with the students talking about the Westward Movement. This included viewing video clips, examining photographs from that period, and generating class conversation and student questions. For beginning to intermediate English learners who are facing the double cognitive load described earlier, the teacher may consider reading the textbook as an add-on to support up-front discussion. Textbooks also include nontextual information that can serve as a springboard for discussion, such as photos, graphs, charts, and other non–language-based graphics to support understanding (see Figure 6.2).

Provide Multiple Passes and Processes

This construct refers to offering students repeated opportunities to access and understand important information. Additionally, rather than simply repeating information in the same way (e.g., reading a passage several times), students should be able to take repeated passes in ways that vary the processing mode (e.g., sketching out a key concept or enacting a historical event).

Multiple Passes

Doing any task just once is not enough to become proficient at it. Repeatedly performing a task helps develop ease and competence. Multiple exposures and multiple opportunities to practice and process information are critical for English learners. Claude Goldenberg (2008) refers to this as "redundant key information." Examples of multiple passes at information include the following:

- manipulating information in some way, such as interpreting results, writing observations, creating data charts, maintaining learning logs, and personalizing the information

- reading the material or portions of the material aloud and discussing key points before the students read it by themselves

- showing relevant video clips before the students read the text

- having English language learners read relevant hi-lo texts on the topic at hand and discussing with them before reading the textbook

- talking through visual representations, explanatory or organizational features, and typographical features of the text, as shown in Figure 6.2

Figure 6.2 Text Features That Support Comprehension

Visual Representations	Explanatory or Organizational Features	Typographical Features
A model, photo, diagram, manipulative, or superimposed text box that clarifies, contextualizes, exemplifies, or extends the text's meaning	A table of contents, glossary, and any additional information at the end of the book such as a quiz or list of activities	Italics, bold, color coding, underlining, headings, or subheadings

Printed with permission from Ruth Yopp

Choral Reading

Group or choral reading models the rhythms and cadences of English. It allows students to hear how words are pronounced and how they fit in the flow of written language. Students may join in to the extent they feel comfortable. If listening, students are simultaneously receiving visual and aural input, dual exposure, and opportunities to process and learn language.

Graphic Novels

Graphic novels are text, both fiction and expository, in comic book format. The format alone appeals to students. For English language learners, combining text and images provides for a great deal of comprehensible input. Through the graphics, the language that is used is contextualized, supported, and expanded beyond just the text in the following ways:

- Facial expressions can convey a gamut of emotions.

- Text is broken into more manageable "chunks."

- Both the typographics (e.g., bold or jagged lettering, or italics) and the shape of the dialogue bubbles in which the text appears convey meaning.

- The images provide information that make drawing conclusions more obvious.

Increasing numbers of graphic books are available. Graphic novels that focus on historical events and people have the advantage of depicting periods of history with augmented meaning through historically accurate clothing and modes of transportation. Some use panel divisions to make jumps in history or varying perspectives more obvious. Some graphic novels add sidebars or pictures of historical documents (Boerman-Cornell 2013). Others tell stories of mathematicians' lives and model their mathematical thinking, problem solving, and equations as part of the graphics as they are working through concepts that they are puzzling over (Boerman-Cornell 2013). Other graphic novels take students through the scientific processes of observation as scientists work through their theories and experiments, again supported by graphic depictions. The following is a brief list of graphic novels that support math and science instruction in meaningful ways:

- *Logicomix* by Apostolos Doxiadis, Christos H. Papadimitriou, Alecos Papadatos, and Annie Di Donna

- *T-Minus, Two-Fisted Science: Stories About Scientists, Suspended in Language,* and other titles by Jim Ottaviani

- *Clan Apis, The Sandwalk Adventures,* and *Optical Allusions* by Jay Hosler

Web Quests

A web quest is an inquiry-based learning format in which the information that students seek and read comes from the Internet. Key elements of a web quest are the introduction, the tasks that are assigned to the students, the process or steps that the students follow in order to complete the tasks, the teacher's preselected resources from which the students search in order to gather research and respond to questions, an evaluation of their work that typically includes a posted rubric of expectations, and a conclusion. Web quests

- involve collaborative, small-group work and division of responsibilities among the group;

- are built on preselected sources located by the teacher so that students spend their time reading and synthesizing relevant information rather than searching; and

- can be developed to take as little time as a day or two to complete, or can be so complex and involved that they can take as long as several weeks to complete.

Students must make decisions about the usefulness and appropriateness of a variety of online sources and texts preselected by the teacher. Students must make choices about discovering information in their own ways, so they are able to respond to the teacher-generated queries and assignments that are posted under the task. They must synthesize their newly gained knowledge in coherent ways, giving them ownership of the content they are writing about. For these reasons, students have opportunities to engage in multiple passes and processes in interacting with and learning about a given topic.

For more information and resources on web quests, visit their website (http://webquest.org).

Multiple Processes

Teachers know that development in one of the four language arts—listening, speaking, reading, and writing—supports and contributes to development in the others. Engaging English language learners in ways to listen, speak, read, and write about information is essential. In the following teaching vignette, English learners work with fluent English speakers in small groups, listening and speaking to complete a task. Good English language modeling by fluent speakers helps English learners improve speaking and listening skills. The following teaching vignette also shows that students carefully reread text together to verify information (since the class had already read the material in the days prior to this review activity). The vignette and the strategy the teacher used, True–False–Fix It, fully demonstrates the construct of multiple passes and processes.

As a review activity for a unit of study about the early development of the United States as a nation, Jasmine gave her students a list of ten statements about the economic systems that were in place in the colonies during that period. Students were arranged in small working groups, with the English learners distributed throughout. In these small groups, students read each statement to decide if it was true or false, checking in the social studies text to verify answers. They then had to sort the statements into two piles accordingly, true or false. Once the groups completed the true or false sort, they discussed the statements as a whole group in determining true and false statements. Students were then instructed to return to the false statements and modify them to change them to true statements.

Printed with permission from Jasmine Barragán

This small-group activity and whole-group processing provided several passes and means of processing the social studies material, including opportunities to talk about it, reread material about it, and write short pieces about it.

Seek and Use Primary-Language Support

A great deal of research indicates that primarylanguage support is useful for helping English learners with content instruction (Goldenberg 2008; August and Shanahan 2006). Indirectly, it also lends support to English language learning. By understanding a concept, term, or vocabulary word in the student's primary language, and then hearing, seeing, reading, or saying it in English, the student more easily grasps the meaning, as well as learning how to express it in English. Primary-language support should be as equally encouraged and valued as other learning resources.

As a point of clarification, continual translation is never recommended. Ongoing translation is very different from primary-language support. Continual translation is not effective because it takes away the motivation to work at negotiating meaning in English. Translation brings about dependency on a language broker. Primary-language support should be viewed as a temporary learning scaffold while developing English language skills. Negotiating meaning is necessary. It should be a joint venture between the learner and teacher, and it implies effort and engagement from both parties. Active learning means full engagement and effort, which translation does not promote.

There are three common sources for primary-language support. In addition, structuring the use of primary-language support in the classroom is an important aspect of its effective use.

1. **The teacher may know students' primary language**, or enough to provide key vocabulary or concepts. In this case, the preview/review strategy explained in Chapter 5 is effective. Note that this strategy should be used only if the English learners have one common primary language. Even if the teacher happens to speak several languages, it becomes unwieldy to provide previews in multiple languages. This strategy gives English learners an overview of the key concepts and vocabulary of the material in the primary language. The preview portion of the strategy can be thought of as front-loading in the primary language. When time permits only a preview or review, a preview is preferable since front-loading or scaffolding information in advance is generally more effective. This approach provides access to the core curriculum while indirectly supporting English language development. The process includes

   - a five- to ten-minute preview in the primary language;
   - the lesson in English; and
   - a five- to ten-minute review of the lesson's key concepts and vocabulary.

2. **Books and online material in the student's primary language** may be available. Local libraries are excellent sources for other-than-English books, especially if a significant number of speakers of other languages live in the community. Of course, the teacher will want to preview online material, checking for appropriateness by looking through photos and other visual support material on the site. An excellent learning support is to provide parallel reading material in the student's primary language. For example, for a unit of study on Earth and human activity, locating material in the student's primary

language on Earth's natural resources, how humans impact Earth's systems, and/or global climate change will help provide understanding. The student will be able to study the material in the primary language and learn how to express some of this information in English. (Recall the student discussed in Chapter 2 who had studied biology in Spanish and, based on her prior knowledge, learned English because she already knew many of the important concepts in Spanish. The same principle applies here.)

3. **Bilingual students may be available in the classroom** to provide scaffolding and support. Discussing class material in the primary language should serve to support learning for both students. Providing assistance to another student should never be an unwelcome responsibility for the bilingual student. Two points to consider are as follows:

   - Be specific about what learning tasks the students should jointly do. For example, the teacher can indicate key concepts from the lesson for the students to preview or review, or key vocabulary items to go over.

   - Ensure that the bilingual student experiences equal learning time as other students in the class.

Provide Structured Interactive Learning Opportunities

Promoting interactive and cooperative group learning activities among students provides beneficial opportunities for meaningful and purposeful communication, authentic academic language use, and language modeling for English learners. Student interaction allows for negotiating meaning, an important aspect for English learners (Echevarría and Graves 2011). Small-group learning also provides multiple passes and processes—opportunities to hear and manipulate key information and use combinations of listening, speaking, reading, and writing.

However, teachers must take care to provide appropriate structures within which students can accomplish small-group assignments. According to Claude Goldenberg,

> "Tasks that students engage in must be carefully designed to be instructionally meaningful and provide suitable opportunities for students to participate at their functional level. Simply pairing or grouping students together and encouraging them to interact or help each other is not sufficient."
>
> —Claude Goldenberg (2008, 21)

In addition to task and time frame, many teachers assign specific roles and responsibilities. In this connection, however, Goldenberg points out that students may not know how to work with, or include, English learners (2008). The two strategies outlined in the sections that follow address this point.

Prepped Partner

In every group of students, there are usually at least a few who are particularly nurturing, or who may be teachers in the making. Even brief instruction for these students on how to engage with and support English language learners is valuable. Instruction in preparing partners can include teaching them to

- ask simple or simplified questions;
- ensure that the group members give enough wait time for the English learner to answer;
- supply words when the student is casting around for the right term; and
- ensure that the group recognizes contributions from the English language learner.

Pairings

This strategy pairs a beginning-to-intermediate English speaker with a fluent English speaker. Both are assigned the same role or responsibility in a group. This allows the English learner to participate in the group without carrying the full responsibility for the learning task, to receive language modeling, and to have multiple passes at understanding language.

Applicable to many small-group assignments, this strategy can be especially effective for literature group studies. The pair can do shared or ear-to-ear reading, allowing for discussion of unclear portions of the text prior to the literature circle meeting.

Small-Group Considerations

In addition to the suggestions in the preceding sections, there are three final considerations. Arrange for a variety of small groups for a variety of purposes with varying group membership throughout the school year. This assures equal learning opportunities for all students. Arranging for rotating group roles (materials manager, recorder, timekeeper) that are commensurate with language levels is also important. Finally, English learners should not be grouped together by language level, except for specific ELD/ESL instruction. That is, there should be an equitable distribution of beginning, intermediate, and advanced English learners in each group, to the greatest extent possible. This helps with language modeling and keeps the group moving forward on the academic task at hand.

Use Direct Instruction Strategies to Promote Reading Comprehension

Substantial research shows that with effective direct instruction, English learners are able to perform equally as well as fluent English speakers at sound and word-level tasks: phonological skills, letter-sound combinations, decoding, word recognition, and spelling (August and Shanahan 2006; Goldenberg 2008). However, research also reveals that reading comprehension is an area in which far too many English learners fall woefully behind. Goldenberg suggests that "when the language requirements are relatively low," it is easier to make adequate progress (Goldenberg 2008, 22). However, as both the reading material and the language used to express it become increasingly sophisticated, overall language demands increase significantly. A reader must be relatively proficient at language to understand and apply comprehension strategies such as think-alouds, the predict-question-clarify-summarize approach, and question-answer relationships (QAR; "right there, put together, on my own, writer and me"). Thus, it is not surprising that English learners are greatly challenged in putting these comprehension strategies to use.

Recall that English learners need patterns, structure, and direct instruction to help them navigate a new language. They have not yet developed an intuitive sense of grammatical patterns, language nuances, or text structures, and they often lack sufficient vocabulary knowledge. Their working memory may well be taken up with lower levels of language tasks such as sounding out words and seeking definitions. It is likely that not until the beginning-advanced level will an English learner become proficient enough to begin to devote the needed attention to comprehension. For English learners, strategies like finding the main idea or doing a think-aloud, for example, do not contain enough structure or direct information to guide them. They need tighter scaffolding, narrower focus, smaller language steps, and more direct instruction.

Statements formed as commands are direct. They are short, carry a clear meaning, and require action (e.g., "Sit there," "Pick this up"). Teaching English learners short and specific tasks to accomplish when they read is effective. These can be thought of as *segue strategies* to be used until English learners are ready to use comprehension strategies that fluent English speakers use. The usefulness of segue strategies lies in the direct language and direct instruction they provide English learners.

Figures 6.3 and 6.4 detail twelve segue strategies—practical direct instruction strategies stated in the form of commands that can help English learners process text and read for meaning. Some of the strategies are similar in intent to those that teachers use with fluent English students. For example, "Tell Myself What I Know" and "Ask a Question" are similar to the first two steps in the familiar and commonly used survey, question, clarify, and review. Stated in command form, the strategies are tangible and sufficiently structured for English learners. There are other strategies that fluent English speakers likely do not need but English learners do because of their limited knowledge of English. Two examples are "Scan and Chunk" and "Look for Extras." English learners need to be taught to become skilled at gleaning information and comprehension in multiple ways that include mining word knowledge and non-text-based information.

Fluent English speakers need to be taught comprehension strategies, have them repeatedly modeled, and practice them in order to begin to use them as independent readers. Similarly for English learners, each strategy described in Figure 6.3 needs to be taught, repeatedly modeled, learned, and applied. It's most beneficial to start from the first strategy and gradually add them. For example, "Scan and Chunk" is an important step to take before "Ask a Question." This is because the phrases and pieces of language the student recognizes in the text will help him or her think about what is known and familiar. This information can help the student formulate a question that he or she may have about the topic. Similarly, a student should "Look Around" and "Read It Again" before "Guess and Skip" and "Pinpoint and Ask." Completing the first step ("Look Around") means that the student will first seek additional input. The first two steps ("Look Around" and "Read It Again") mean that the student will have taken some initiative and responsibility, and will have a better chance to make a reasonable guess prior to "Guess and Skip." Completing the first three steps ("Look Around," "Read It Again," "Guess and Skip") means that the student will have invested effort into making sense of the text prior to Pinpoint and Ask.

Many of these segue strategies parallel the Common Core State Standards. For example, "Check for Extras" pairs well with Standard R.7 of the College and Career Readiness Anchor Standards for Reading, "Integrate and evaluate content presented in diverse media and formats, including visually and quantitatively, as well as in words" (CCSSO 2010, 10). Another example is "Put the Pieces Together," which parallels Standard R.5: "Analyze the structure of texts, including how specific sentences, paragraphs, and larger portions of the text (e.g., a section, chapter, scene, or stanza) relate to each other and the whole" (CCSSO 2010, 10).

Figure 6.3 Segue Strategies: Direct Instruction Strategies that Promote Reading Comprehension for English Language Learners

Before I Read	Teacher's Note
Check for extras. What are the extra visual clues that I can use?	Teach the student to "read" all available visual, explanatory, and typographical information before reading the text. Refer to the chart in the "Provide Multiple Passes and Processes" section.
Scan and chunk. What vocabulary, patterns, and pieces of language "chunks" do I know? I find them before I read. I know I will have some "word friends" when I read them in the text.	This is self-motivating positive reinforcement even before the student starts to read. It provides a starting point that the reader can build from.
Tell myself what I know. Think about what I already know about the topic.	Reminding students to help themselves recall any information they may already have about the topic is an established important step for all readers.
Ask a question. What do I want to find out about in this text?	Even just one question is a good starting point.
When I Read	**Teacher's Note**
Look around. When I come to words or phrases that I don't know, what can I find on the pages in front of me that can help me understand? A graph? A photo? A caption? A definition?	Why are the same two pages of the book open? Novice readers have a relatively "short fuse" when it comes to flipping through multiple pages seeking information. It can be discouraging and difficult to know when to stop flipping and seeking. Keeping eyes on the same page focuses a reader. A more mature reader and more proficient English learner will learn to add more pages to the seeking process.

When I Read	Teacher's Note
Read it again. If I have trouble reading a sentence or a paragraph, I can read it again to see if it starts to make more sense.	Rereading is always a good idea.
Guess and skip. After I've looked around on the page, and I've reread it, I make the best guess I can with what I have been able to figure out. I keep reading.	Making considered and educated guesses can prevent a student from getting bogged down or giving up.
Pinpoint and ask. When I get lost in too many words and too much language that I can't understand, I can ask someone about specific words or phrases or a few sentences.	This strategy teaches a student that saying "I don't get it" is not helpful because it is too general for anyone to be able to explain or describe something. Much more helpful for the reader and "explainer" is to focus and make a specific reference or ask a specific question.
After I Read	**Teacher's Note**
Tell it to myself. Tell myself what I read, doing the best that I can. I can look back at what I read to help myself. Did I find the answer to my question? What is the answer?	Retelling is a first step in summarizing. Asking a reader to say or write what he or she remembers from the text is more direct and less daunting than selecting and synthesizing the main points.
Put the pieces together. What "pieces" of what I read helped me understand this text?	This step helps students begin to process increasingly larger pieces of the text. Are there pieces of related text in the reader's mind? Did a certain paragraph help explain a graph, photograph, or subtitle? Are there sentences or paragraphs that explain or outline a process or sequence of events? How did the student make sense of larger pieces of text to learn more?

Figure 6.4 presents two more strategies that can be woven into either "When I Read" or "After I Read." These are helpful for more advanced English learners and older students who won't get bogged down in a great number of strategies, or for those who have internalized some strategies and are ready to work on new ones. A teacher may also find either of these strategies to be more helpful, and he or she may want to substitute one, for one or two of the others listed in Figure 6.3.

Figure 6.4 Additional Segue Strategies for Advanced English Language Learners

Additional When I Read and After I Read Strategies	Teacher's Note
Read and write. Write what I learned.	A student should be encouraged to take notes—phrases, questions, and comments—while reading or immediately afterward. This provides two processing modes as discussed in the "Provide Multiple Passes and Processes" section and gives the reader a chance to capture and revisit what he or she felt was important to write down during the reading process. It also gives a teacher the opportunity to review what a student has understood.
Sketch it out. Sketch what I learned.	The term *sketch*, rather than *draw*, more intentionally captures a preliminary image or thought about something, as an artist's sketch. English learners should be encouraged to make visual representations of what they understand, to add explanatory text as they are able, and to modify and expand supporting text as they increasingly understand the concepts. Further, sketching activates another way of processing information. "Seeing" what the student understands is also a way that a teacher can assess a student's comprehension. This can lead to correcting or modifying any misunderstanding or lack of clarity.

Direct instruction to promote reading comprehension in the form of these twelve segue strategies can promote English learners' reading for understanding.

Summary

Making meaning tangible is essential for English language learners. This can include making abstract ideas more concrete by making meaning visible and accessible in a number of ways, as discussed in this chapter. Primary language support is another essential meaning-making support. Providing multiple passes and processes and interactive learning are effective classroom-based approaches that support and build comprehension. Finally, teaching students strategies that help them build their own toolbox of reading skills is critical. These include direct instruction about language patterns and structures, and teaching students to use segue comprehension strategies. Embedding elements of the eight constructs discussed in this chapter into instruction in a variety of ways is constructive in helping English language learners become successful readers.

Apply, Reflect, and Extend

1. Think of a series of lessons you have recently taught or will teach that present students with abstract concepts. List two of these concepts. How can you "unpack" these concepts to make meaning visible and comprehensible for English language learners?

2. What additional series books do you know of that are appropriate for your grade level and that present students with common structures? What types of structures do they provide?

3. For a current or upcoming unit of study, locate a web quest that might be appropriate for English language learners and fluent English speakers working together in a small group. Consider building a web quest to support upcoming instruction.

4. Find some online text in a language in which you are not proficient. Apply some of the segue strategies described in this chapter. Then, think metacognitively about your reading process. How did these strategies work?

5. Introduce and model one or two segue strategies with English language learners. Have them actively use these for one week. Record their progress.

Chapter 7

Teaching Writing

Anticipatory Quiz

Are the following statements true or false?

_____ 1. Helping English learners develop writing skills is fundamentally different from guiding fluent English speakers in developing this aspect of language.

_____ 2. Informative/explanatory and narrative discourse are good starting points for beginning language learners.

_____ 3. A student's level of oral proficiency in English is generally a good indication of writing ability.

_____ 4. Long-term English language learners have generally developed the necessary level of academic English to support clear writing.

_____ 5. Open sorts provide a nonlinguistic way of demonstrating logical thinking and a basis for argumentative writing.

_____ 6. Intermediate-level English language learners should begin to practice on-demand writing to prompts and questions.

In her book about writing, *Bird by Bird*, author Anne Lamott (1995) describes a scene from her childhood. One evening her brother broke down crying, confessing he had a research report on birds due the next day at school. He had not written one word of it. Their dad, an author and teacher, clapped his hand on the boy's shoulder and said, "Son, just take it bird by bird."

For many, writing is the most challenging of the four domains of language. What makes writing so challenging—even intimidating? One reason is that speaking and writing are productive language skills, and as such, they can require more effort than the receptive skills of listening and reading. Another reason is that even though speaking is a productive language skill, it allows for pauses, think time, and "take backs" (e.g., "What I really mean to say is…"). Writing, however, does not permit these. It can be challenging to gather random thoughts and commit them to an orderly and sense-making discourse. Writing is also a solitary endeavor. Apart from sharing ideas with someone or receiving feedback, individual effort and focus are required to shape written discourse. Writing requires applied knowledge of the mechanics of grammar and syntax, as well as an "ear" for the art of creating a logical and pleasing flow of ideas and language. Moreover, putting something in writing can be intimidating because it is there for everyone to see—mistakes and all. Speech is the primary and fundamental source of communication, and a human universal. Writing is a secondary form of discourse, and therefore one step removed from what comes naturally to us.

There are fundamental truths that apply to all writers. The next section describes the ten commonly held truths about writing. Following this is a section offering ten tips for teaching writing to English language learners. The final section provides strategies and approaches to help English language learners develop writing abilities.

Ten Truths about Writing

The principles of writing discussed here provide a base of understanding prior to considering particular needs for helping English language learners improve their writing abilities.

Writing Ability Develops Incrementally

The more writers practice, and the more guidance and feedback they receive, the better their writing gets. Without practice and direct feedback about how to make their writing better, writers cannot develop their craft to the best of their abilities.

Writers Must Consider Task, Purpose, and Audience

A writer needs to be clear and aware of these elements in shaping every piece of writing, no matter the topic or genre. Word choice and grammatical structure particularly affect audience and purpose. The Common Core Anchor Standard for Range of Writing W.9 explicitly addresses this point: students must "write routinely over extended time frames (time for research, reflection, and revision) and shorter time frames (a single sitting or a day or two) for a range of tasks, purposes, and audiences" (CCSSO 2010, 41).

Writers Need a Connection to Their Topic

Writers bring energy and enthusiasm to a piece of writing through their connection to a topic. A topic about which the writer has something to say often goes hand-in-hand with an authentic reason to write. The authenticity is derived from the desire to express something about that topic. Both of these elements—selecting an appealing topic and having an authentic reason to write—are internally driven reasons for writing, and they are far more compelling than those that are externally driven.

Writers Benefit from Thinking and Talking about Their Ideas

Writers think about what they want to convey and how they will accomplish this. They think about the structure and organization of a piece of writing. Budding writers must often come to understand that what they may read in a minute's time was a long time in the making, even before a word was written or typed. Words do not flow magically from pen to paper or from fingers to keyboard. Good writing reflects a great deal of advance reflection, talking, and thinking.

Writing Builds and Clarifies Thinking

Constructing meaningful discourse requires step-by-step, logical thinking. It requires clear expression of concepts and their relationships to each other, careful description, use of appropriate structures, and precise vocabulary choices. Writing helps students develop higher-order thinking, which is the underlying requirement woven throughout the Common Core State Standards.

Writers Need Opportunities to Write Regularly

Writing is a creative process, but it is also disciplined. The discipline of sitting down regularly to write helps develop the habit, the frame of mind, and the disposition to be able to actively write. Establishing a regular writing time brings about a synergy between creativity and discipline in developing writing fluency.

Fluency and Form Work Together in Writing

Ease in generating ideas and writing them down makes a writer fluent. Form requires many additional "comb-throughs." Fluency is the initial goal, because once the important ideas are captured, it is possible to work through and shape the rest. Form, then, includes rearranging ideas, emphasizing certain points with just the right descriptions, ensuring grammatical correctness, and adjusting vocabulary, among many other aspects. Fluency is the first key goal.

The Writing Process Involves a Number of Steps

The writing process consists of interconnected steps of prewriting or brainstorming, drafting, revising, editing, and finally publishing (although a writer never stops thinking about how to improve a piece of writing even after it is published). Except for publishing, the stages do not necessarily occur in a linear order. For example, a writer can brainstorm, then write a draft, then brainstorm some more, then revise a portion, and then revise the draft. However, for young writers, the writing process is a helpful framework to follow. It provides a good mental model and develops understanding that every writer passes through these stages when developing written discourse. Good writing does not occur without effort and reworking.

Writers Pay Attention to Other Writers' Work

The more a writer reads or is read to, the better his or her writing becomes. It is essential for young writers to focus on, think about, and discuss what makes a particular piece of writing good. Writers get ideas from others about topics, language, writing techniques, and more through hearing and discussing well-written language.

Writers Enjoy Having Their Work Published

Every writer derives great satisfaction from seeing his or her work published. In the classroom, this could mean binding a simple, clean, final edit of students' work. Teachers should provide publishing opportunities to their students. In addition to the satisfaction students derive from publishing their work, it also serves as a stimulus for further writing.

Ten Tips for Teaching Writing to English Language Learners

Although fundamental truths about writing apply to all writers, there are particular considerations to keep in mind that pertain to English language learners. Mastering writing in a second language takes effort and time—by some estimates, it can take anywhere from five to eight years or more to become proficiently literate in English. This is not unreasonable, given that native English speakers require about the same amount of time. In fact, it is the rare native-English-speaking fifth grader who has mastered the ability to write proficiently. English learners most commonly experience the greatest challenges with writing, and it is typically the last language domain to be perfected. A teacher's regular writing instruction and encouragement, and the student's effort and practice, are the key ingredients for improving a student's writing.

The sections that follow discuss these considerations within the context of the requirements set by the CCSS College and Career Readiness (CCR) Anchor Standards for Writing. The three text types emphasized in the Common Core are opinion/arguments, informative/explanatory, and narratives. Writing arguments can be challenging for English learners due to the abstract nature of logical thinking that is conveyed through written language. However, at about the intermediate level, students should begin practicing to support their claims through the use of data and other verifiable text-based information. Informative/explanatory and narrative discourse are more within the writing range of late-beginning and intermediate-level students. This is because informative/explanatory text tends to be expressed in concrete language (especially in the sciences), which is more easily understood and expressed than abstract language. Narrative discourse, organized around a plot or logical sequence of events and standard story elements, is a common format that many students have been repeatedly exposed to and are very familiar with. Therefore, either informative/explanatory or narrative text serves as a good starting point for beginning to intermediate students.

It is essential that all English learners, to the extent that their language abilities permit, support their own learning through writing journals and reports, organizing data, taking notes, and in general manipulating information in written form. This type of writing fits well with the Common Core requirement that students write over short time-frames. At the late-intermediate level of English, students should begin to have opportunities to do extended writing over several days that include time for research, reflection, and revisions. Academic writing relies on the ability to respond to prompts using text-based evidence and examples, to analyze text through close reading, to draw conclusions, and to synthesize material from several sources. This type of writing requires language sophistication that intermediate-level students should begin to practice and engage in. The Anchor Standards for Writing at the fourth-grade level include a balance of types of writing that reflect about 35 percent narrative, 35 percent informative/explanatory, and 30 percent argumentative, providing guidelines for instruction and for classroom-based writing opportunities (CCSSO 2010).

The Common Core Anchor Standards for Writing will appear throughout the following sections, with specific points to help teachers think about English language learners' writing development in the context of the standards.

Foster Writing for Text Types and Purposes

College and Career Readiness Anchor Standards for Writing: Text Types and Purposes

- Write arguments to support claims in an analysis of substantive topics or texts using valid reasoning and relevant and sufficient evidence.

- Write informative/explanatory texts to examine and convey complex ideas and information clearly and accurately through the effective selection, organization, and analysis of content.

- Write narratives to develop real or imagined experiences or events using effective techniques, well-chosen details, and well-structured event sequences.

—CCSSO (2010, 18)

It is a challenge for beginning-level English language learners to understand or produce writing beyond words and phrases. At the late-beginning and intermediate levels, however, teachers should begin to point out, talk about, and provide examples for the three different types of writing: argumentative, informative/explanatory, and narrative. Starting with either clear informative/explanatory text or simple stories is recommended. This is because the nature and language of a story and the nature of simple and clearly written explanatory text can be made evident. Asking beginning- and intermediate-level students to read and respond to informative/explanatory text taken from hi-lo readers is a good choice.

Argumentative text requires close reading and support of a claim or a main idea, which requires some sophistication with language skills. It is, therefore, a writing task more successfully undertaken by students with some English language facility. Beginning in the fourth grade, the Common Core State Standards require argumentative writing (2010). The "Writing Strategies for English Learners" section, in this chapter, offers examples and ideas on ways to introduce argumentative writing to English learners.

Provide Support for Writing Tasks

Support and direct instruction are important for all writers; however, direct guidance and specific instruction using patterns, structures, models, scaffolds, and organization techniques are even more important for English language learners. These types of writing supports are useful because it is easy to get tangled up in ideas and concepts, and not to know where to start. For example, sentence frames provide a structure into which students may insert information and a starting point from which to expand. "*X* rest during the day because ____." and "After we ____, we need to be sure to ____ because ____." are sentence frame examples. Graphic organizers with small amounts of text provide a tangible structure and can offer a logical starting point for English language learners.

Provide Extensive Vocabulary Scaffolding and Support

As is the case with reading, English language learners need a great deal of assistance with vocabulary development and usage. A visually print-rich classroom environment featuring word walls, charts, posters of unit vocabulary, and posted lists of high-frequency words can help. Oral discussion helps every writer. As part of pre-discussion and brainstorming, providing the key vocabulary in advance of writing offers an important scaffold.

Use Oral Proficiency as a Guide for Writing Proficiency

Consider the student's level of oral English proficiency as a general guide for the level of writing to expect. Use the Student Oral Language Observation Matrix described in Chapter 2 as a starting resource. However, there is an important caveat: although long-term English learners' spoken English is sufficient for everyday social conversation, and their speech may seem relatively proficient and smooth, most have not developed the necessary level of fluent academic English to support school success. Long-term English learners are students in grades 6–12 who have been continually enrolled in school in the United States more than six years, and who have not met the criteria for reclassification. According to Laurie Olsen (2010), about 59 percent of the English learner population in grades

6–12 in California, and about 34 percent in New York City, are long-term English learners. Obtaining writing samples from such students on a general academic topic can reveal their ease with, and ability to produce, fluent academic writing.

Consider Native Language Writing Ability

Consider the student's native language writing proficiency and level of formal schooling to help determine English language writing abilities. The more advanced the student's writing in the native language, the more aptly he or she will be able to transfer to writing in English. Also, examining the student's writing in English may give clues about writing awareness and ability in the areas of text organization, sentence variety, and conventions of writing, as the following example shows.

(Original Work)

One day ther was a littler chicken. The littler chichen was walking. the something hit on her head. Then the chicken little jell – "The sky is fallyn" she said.

The coming other chicken – "waht is the matter" – she said.

"the sky is fallyn" said the chicken little. "call the police" – she said.

thes is my laky day – said the wolf.

(Interpretation)

One day there was a little chicken. The little chicken was walking. Then something hit on her head. Then, Chicken Little yelled, "The sky is falling," she said.

There was coming [an]other chicken. "What is the matter" she said.

"The sky is falling" said the Chicken Little. "Call the police" – she said.

This is my lucky day – said the wolf.

Notice that this student includes both the English (quotation marks) and the Spanish (dashes) forms of indicating speech. This student already understands that writers need to indicate direct speech; therefore, he just requires a bit of fine-tuning on the use of quotation marks in English, rather than direct instruction and practice on the use of quotation marks. He writes in complete sentences and uses periods. His writing also demonstrates that he has a clear sense of story progression. The general sense from this writing sample is that this student has a solid grounding in literacy in his first language that provides support in learning to write in English. It is worth the teacher's further exploration to assess his ability to write informative/explanatory and even argumentative/persuasive text.

Provide Collaborative Online Writing Opportunities

College and Career Readiness Anchor Standards for Writing: Production and Distribution of Writing

Use technology, including the Internet, to produce and publish writing and to interact and collaborate with others.

—CCSSO (2010, 41)

Collaborative writing is a natural fit with technology integration (Kist 2013). Michael Dappolone (2013) points out that students who make just short posts on blogs or wikis are using their writing abilities, and it is then not such a leap to learn to write lengthier discourse and to write for additional purposes. Having students develop and contribute to wikis and blogs certainly addresses the issues of writing collaboratively and for authentic purposes. Digital reading and writing parallel students' use of literacy in their personal lives. Writing in these online venues provides a natural entrée to practicing and improving their writing and reading skills that serves them well in today's increasingly digital world.

Provide Provisional Writing Opportunities

College and Career Readiness Anchor Standards for Writing: Range of Writing

Write routinely over extended time frames (time for research, reflection, and revision) and shorter time frames (a single sitting or a day or two) for a range of tasks, purposes, and audiences.

—CCSSO (2010, 41)

The Common Core State Standards require students to use reading and writing to build thinking skills by seeking and organizing information. English learners need to do provisional writing that supports immediate learning. Provisional writing is a type of scaffold that serves a purpose for the time being. It can subsequently be expanded upon or improved upon as needed. Examples are learning logs describing processes, procedures, and how and why things work, such as found in scientific writing and consequences and outcomes, as is often used in the social sciences. Provisional writing can also help students capture ideas that can be improved upon and turned into more polished written discourse. Provisional writing

- helps students manipulate, organize, and therefore derive better understanding of material;

- helps teachers assess students' understanding and areas for improvement;

- is less intimidating and less formal than on-demand writing, such as writing in responses to prompts or test questions;

- is an intermediate step to more polished writing; and

- is a bridge between brief writing assignments and more sustained and research-based writing assignments requiring the use of various sources.

Offer On-Demand Writing Opportunities

English learners should begin to practice on-demand writing from the intermediate stage of language development. This requires a great deal of direct instruction and modeling. On-demand writing requires, for example, that students demonstrate the ability to compare, contrast, support, justify, analyze, or make an argument for something in writing. Starting each class session or each day with a focused five- to ten-minute quick write on a prompt that addresses a "big idea" accomplishes the following three goals:

- It establishes a regular writing time (as discussed previously).

- It gets students thinking, and writing, about big ideas.

- It gets students accustomed to using one of the emphasized verbs in the Common Core (*compare, contrast, support, make an argument for*, etc.).

Conduct Writing Conferences with Students

Writing conferences with students need a specific focus. An English learner can quickly become overwhelmed and discouraged with rewriting, editing, and grammar or vocabulary instruction overload. Start by focusing on meaning, and describe what the writer does well. Then, for example, the conference may be an appropriate time to address a specific point of grammar or to provide direct instruction on the semantic nuances of a word or phrase the student has written. It is important to limit the purpose of a writing conference to one or two points.

Offer Specific Feedback on Writing

English learners cannot rely on native speaker intuition. Native English speakers generally have an innate sense that tells them when something is not correct or does not flow well. More specific types of feedback are necessary for English language learners to help them discern when a piece of writing is not quite right, and to help them understand what needs attention. While the Common Core State Standards expect that students will "revisit and make improvements to a piece of writing over multiple drafts" (CCSSO 2010, 41), English learners will require assistance in editing and fine-tuning written discourse until they have fully developed English language proficiency.

Writing Strategies for English Learners

In consideration of the three types of writing that the CCSS require—narrative, informative/explanatory, and argumentative—the following sections outline strategies that promote writing development for beginning, intermediate, and advanced levels of English learners. Repeated modeling and practice promote writing development. Several strategies are applicable to both narrative and informative/explanatory writing. Note that strategies listed as appropriate for a particular level of student can often be used effectively for adjacent levels of English learners.

Beginning Writers

Basic language patterns and a great deal of vocabulary assistance are especially important at this level. The ability of beginning-level English learners to produce writing is limited. They start with copying and writing short phrases. The focus at this stage is to simply encourage students to have the confidence to begin writing in their second language.

Figure 7.1 shows the text types and suggestions for associated activities for beginning writers.

Figure 7.1 Activities for Beginning Writers by Text Type

Text Type	Activities
Narrative	• Life murals • Pattern books • Pattern poetry • Postcards • Story captions • Wordless picture books
Informative/Explanatory	• ABC concept books • Found poetry • Grammatical big books • Grammatical category pattern sentences • Lists and maps • Timelines and cycles • Virtual language experience approach
Argumentative (logical thinking)	• Open sorts

Life Murals

Writing captions and short phrases that accompany drawings or photos of important events that occurred in their lives or creating captioned photo-autobiographies are good writing options for students at this stage. The students' memories and photos provide writing scaffolds as they seek words and phrases to describe their experiences.

Pattern Books

These books provide patterns in which students can add their own words to create both oral and written language. Bill Martin Jr. and Eric Carle's *Brown Bear, Brown Bear, What Do You See?* classic pattern book is just one that students can listen to repeatedly and follow up with by creating their own sentences using this basic pattern.

Pattern Poetry

Patterns and repetition found in poetry provide excellent scaffolding for students learning to write in English, and they offer many possibilities for vocabulary development. Starting slowly, building up, and providing repeated examples for students are important. The students should have time to edit their own work and each other's work, to the extent that their use of English permits. Creative and imaginative thinking grow by spending ample time in the prewriting phase, as shown in the following teaching vignette.

Karyn's third graders were doing a literature unit on *Tom Thumb*. The students were discussing the giant's bad mood. Karyn expanded the discussion by asking the students to think and then talk about their own reasons for good moods and bad moods. As the students provided reasons, she wrote the phrases the students generated on the board. She then asked the students to write poems about their good and bad moods. She wrote this sentence frame on the board for them to use:

I get in a bad mood when ____.

> But ____ makes me smile.
>
> Each of the students wrote several stanzas and selected their favorites, and then Karyn created a class book titled *Bad Moods, Good Moods.*
>
> (Zuñiga–Hill and Yopp 1996)

Figure 7.2 shows four poetry patterns.

Figure 7.2 Poetry Patterns

Pattern	Examples
Five-line sensory poem	Love looks like ____? Love sounds like ____? Love feels like ____. Love smells like ____. Love tastes like ____.
Five-line metaphor poem based on a single idea	Happiness is (a sunset). Happiness is (my mom's perfume). Happiness is (the beach). Happiness is (cookies after school). Happiness is (slides and swings).
I like to … I love to	I like to ____. I like to ____. I like to ____. I like to ____. I like to ____. But I really love to ____.
I used to …	I used to be a ____, but now I'm ____.

Finally, cinquains and diamantes offer two more common poetry patterns that provide writing scaffolds. They also allow students to practice using particular parts of speech, and they help develop vocabulary. Figure 7.3 shows a sample of both patterns.

Figure 7.3 Cinquain and Diamante Poetry Patterns

Cinquain	Diamante (Written in the Shape of a Diamond)
One-word topic Two adjectives Three verbs ending with *-ing* Four-word phrase One word that is a synonym for the first word	**Noun** Two adjectives Three verbs ending with *-ing* Four adjectives Three verbs ending with *-ing* Two adjectives Noun
Trees Green, refreshing Swaying, growing, standing They give us shade. Arbor	**Friend** Constant, kind Writing, creating, sharing Patient, dedicated, trusting, energetic Hoping, waiting, trying, thinking Focused, musical Friend

Postcards

Postcards offer visual scaffolds for writing. The teacher can provide descriptive vocabulary of the visuals presented on the postcards, and students can write brief notes about their imaginary adventures to their family and friends. At the same time, postcards also depict real scenes, and therefore give students opportunities to learn to use language to describe real places, such as beautiful purple mountains, a quiet lake, a starry night, and so on. Students can also be given opportunities to select a picture from a magazine and glue a sheet of paper on the back to create a large postcard on which to write a message.

Story Captions

Story captions can be written after multiple readings of a story. Photocopied pictures from the book can be provided, and the students can sequence these. Then they can write simple sentences that describe the story. For example, after the teacher has read *The Three Little Pigs* to students a few times, followed by discussion, students can create captions such as "This pig used straw," "This pig used sticks," and "The wolf is mean and hungry."

Wordless Picture Books

Wordless picture books provide two types of writing scaffolds. First, much of the necessary vocabulary is evident in the pictures and can be provided to the students as part of the discussion that builds up to the writing process. Second, the structure or story line is also provided through the picture sequences. Students can first discuss the story to generate ideas and language. This oral language then leads to creating simple sentences that describe the depicted story.

ABC Concept Books

Conveying information accurately can be expressed through ABC books that are based on a unit of study. Photocopies of images can be made from textbooks or downloaded from the Internet so that students spend time productively by writing, rather than making pictures.

Figure 7.4 shows an example of what the first letters of an ABC book on the study of geological processes might look like.

Figure 7.4 Sample from The ABC Book of Geology

A	B	C
Active processes change the earth.	Big idea: Earth is very old!	A crust covers the Earth.

Found Poetry

A full description of this activity and student examples appear in Chapter 5. This activity should take place at the end of a unit of study, and it may take several days to complete. It may be more productive to include intermediate-level writers in this activity.

To begin, provide students with a piece of text that includes familiar vocabulary from the unit of study. Read the text with the students. Ask students to read words or phrases that draw their attention. These could be words they know or that they find unusual or interesting in some way. Provide students with strips of paper onto which they can copy their words and phrases. Have students place the strips in a pocket chart. Read through all the words and phrases. Have the students arrange these words and phrases in some way that sounds pleasing to them, through group negotiation. The group must agree on the final arrangement of the words and phrases that make up the poem. This is an excellent way to review familiar vocabulary and concepts.

Grammatical Big Books

To reinforce grammatical concepts and vocabulary, big books can be devoted to one aspect of language or grammar. Examples are *Our Big Book of Opposites*, *Our Big Book of Comparisons* (*-er*, *-est*), or a book containing parts of speech (e.g., verb + *ing*).

Another possibility is to have students create peek-a-boo books by pasting in flaps of paper that conceal pictures and written text of prepositional phrases such as "in the drawer" and "on the desk." For example, students might create a story around these phrases: Tomás lost his soccer ball. He looked everywhere! He looked … (in the closet, in the garbage can). He even looked in…!

Older English learners may write these stories for a younger audience and then read their stories to this audience. They might autograph the book and leave it in the classroom for students to practice reading pattern books.

Grammatical Category Pattern Sentences

Students can create lists with categories of words they learn, such as verbs, adjectives, or prepositional phrases, and use them in patterned sentences. For example:

You're my friend because you're (<u>adjective</u>).

Example: You're my friend because you're fun.

I love you because you're (<u>adjective</u>).

Example: I love you because you're caring.

I'm happy when I'm (<u>verb + *ing*</u>).

Example: I'm happy when I'm playing.

I'm happy when I'm (<u>prepositional phrase</u>).

Example: I'm happy when I'm with my friend.

Students can use this language to create their own simple stories or books.

Lists and Maps

It is common for beginning English language learners to learn new words and phrases based on thematic instruction. Students can use these content words to create lists and maps. An example is the study of an ancient civilization. Using the words they learn, students can make maps of the locations and descriptions of the river systems and physical settings that supported early settlements and civilizations. They can draw maps of principal rivers, showing where products came from and where they were transported to in support of trade.

Timelines and Cycles

Students can use words and phrases to describe a series of events or cycles. Historical events lend themselves well to timelines. Cycles are commonly used to describe particular events that are observed in the natural world, such as the circulatory system and food chains. Pictures can be photocopied from textbooks for students so that their time is spent productively on writing rather than drawing. For example, photos about the events that occurred around the American Revolutionary War can be copied. Students can place the events in the correct chronological order and then write brief phrases that describe the events.

Virtual Language Experience Approach

This is an adaptation of the traditional approach that is based on a commonly shared field trip or similar experience (see Chapter 4). After such an experience, the teacher and students discuss and collectively write about what they learned. In lieu of a field trip, students can watch a video clip on the pertinent area of study. After collectively writing the passage, students can manipulate the sentences and words in a variety of ways to reinforce vocabulary and concepts. For example, they can cut up sentences or phrases and put them back together. The following is an example of a language experience chart that students and a teacher wrote together after watching an introductory video clip about the Earth. The first time the video played, the teacher completely lowered the volume so that students attended only to the visuals. The clip was repeated with volume, so students experienced a cycle of listening, watching, and writing.

We saw billions of stars. We saw a little ball. Then we got closer and closer. It is a place called Earth! It has water, waterfalls, ice, volcanoes, and mountains. It is beautiful! Earth developed billions of years ago. Geologists study Earth. We will study Earth.

Open Sorts

For English learners, argumentative text is the most challenging of the three types of writing because it is typically a more abstract form of thinking and requires some level of independent research and/or thinking. Starting simply by focusing on the thinking or logic behind an argument before having to write about it can give English language learners a developing sense of the goal of writing to this purpose.

The process for open sorts begins by giving students a small number of cards that they can group on the basis of their own thinking. This is a way to visually begin the thinking process that is not exclusively language dependent. Once students sort the cards, they can be helped along with the vocabulary and describing the thinking behind the groupings. Discussing the logic with students, or helping them put their own thinking into words, provides the language for students to write simple sentences.

Examples:

The dog and the zebras are with friends. The other animals are all alone.

The snail and the turtle are small animals. The zebra, the dog, and the whale are large animals.

Examples:

These people are happy. They are smiling because they are doing things they like to do.

Two groups of children are at school studying and working at computers. The other people are not in school.

Intermediate Writers

Intermediate writers benefit from scaffolds, models, and writing support that help them expand their vocabulary and literacy skills. They should continue to be supported with a specified daily block of time for ELD/ESL instruction. They should be introduced to the concept of writing for different purposes (narrative, informative/explanatory, and argumentative) with attention to vocabulary that is used for academic purposes—both general and content specific. Having students study root words and affixes, and helping them include this type of vocabulary in their writing and speaking, is beneficial for students at this level of language development.

Figure 7.5 shows the text types and suggestions for associated activities for intermediate writers.

Figure 7.5 Activities for Intermediate Writers by Text Type

Text Type	Activities
Narrative	• Buddy journals • Cause and effect • Retelling familiar stories • Sentence combining • Show, not tell • Story maps
Informative/explanatory	• Content-area big books • Sentence patterns • Sentence shortening • Structured paragraphs
Argumentative	• What? So what? Now what?

Buddy Journals

This is a type of journal maintained between two students who write back and forth to each other. By pairing English learners with fluent English students, the fluent students can model standard written English and expand the vocabulary of the English learners. Buddy journals provide a peer audience and an authentic reason to write and read. They give immediate feedback. Students can generate their own topics of interest, describe events, share opinions, ask questions, and get to know each other. Electronic journals add to the ease of communicating with each other and give students opportunities to do immediate self-editing. An example of a creative use of buddy journals implemented with elementary students is discussed in Chapter 3.

Cause and Effect

Commonly found verbs in the Common Core such as *cite*, *support*, *justify*, and *provide evidence* require students to give reasons for something that is supported by a fact or detail. Cause and effect is a good place to start instruction to help students learn to write to these types of prompts or questions.

Cause and effect can be demonstrated. It is important to show the students what these words mean while using the relevant phrase "cause and effect." For example, students can understand this concept by observing that pushing something off the table makes it fall, or that throwing a rubber ball on the ground causes it to bounce. By helping students do close reading, breaking down the text of a simple story, and ensuring they understand most of the story's vocabulary, they discern cause and effect.

The examples of student work in Figure 7.6 come from intermediate second-grade English learners who did repeated and close reading of a short story with a teacher and were asked to find a cause and effect in the story. (There were many examples of these in the story they read.) With teacher guidance, the students created cause/effect phrases or sentences, and in a few cases, students included temporal words such as *when* and *after*. Students can also practice cause/effect writing with informative/explanatory text.

Figure 7.6 Examples of Student Cause/Effect Work

Cause and Effect	
Student 1	When Officer Buckle saw Gloria do the speeches, he got jealous.
Student 2	Gloria did the speeches and Officer Buckle got mad. So he decided to share his safety tips.
Student 3	Officer Buckle's safety tip #7—never stand on a swivel chair! He did! And so he fell off!

Retelling Familiar Stories

Retelling stories, such as family stories or events, is based on the scaffold of familiarity. Students know their own stories well, and so the learning for them is the vocabulary that they need in order to write the story in English. Students can help themselves by first developing a story map of the event's sequence or important details. Giving students continual practice in retelling familiar stories helps them develop the skills they need to write to the Common Core Anchor Standard for Writing 3; "Write narratives to develop real or imagined experiences or events using effective technique, well-chosen details, and well-structured events" (CCSSO 2010, 41).

Sentence Combining

Many intermediate-level students use the basic sentence pattern of subject-verb-object. They need help becoming familiar with and practicing other patterns. They should be provided with several choppy subject-verb sentences on the same topic, as shown in the following examples, to combine the sentences into more complex and interesting ones. Modeling and repeated practice are important. Working in small groups, students can combine the ideas, and then each small group can share their work with the whole group. The following is an example of choppy subject-verb sentences that students could be asked to combine.

I live on an island. The island is big. The island has lots of plants and animals. It has many tall trees. Plants are everywhere. Animals walk around all over. There are not very many people. I like this island.

Show, Not Tell

This instructional strategy helps English language learners develop vocabulary and descriptive writing skills (Peregoy and Boyle 2013). First, students read a paragraph that is rich in description and paints a picture in their minds. Here is an example:

> Whispers of creatures are all around blowing their nasty breaths on me. Groans and the distant howls of animals fill the air. What's crawling around my feet and legs? Hanging cobwebs brush my face. A deep coldness soaks through my coat. Every path ends where it began. I am scared and lost in the witch's enchanted forest.
>
> *Printed with permission from Zuñiga Dunlap and Marino Weismann 2006*

Compare this paragraph to the following: "I was scared and lost in the witch's forest."

Showing and not telling helps students practice painting a picture with words. Repeated lessons with students that help them begin to show and not tell will strengthen their vocabulary and narrative writing. Starting with a brainstorming session on relevant vocabulary is helpful. Here are five basic sentences, each one providing an opportunity to help students develop "show, not tell" language:

- She didn't have any friends.
- I love my mom.
- Family picnics are so much fun.
- My dog is old.
- That was the scariest moment of my life!

Story Maps

These are graphic representations of the organization of a story that give structural, visual, and mental models. Story maps are postreading and prewriting structures that support students' ability to retell the story in writing. After reading the story to students, the teacher talks through and simultaneously maps out the story. Figure 7.7 shows an example for *The Three Little Pigs*.

Figure 7.7 Sample Story Map of *The Three Little Pigs*

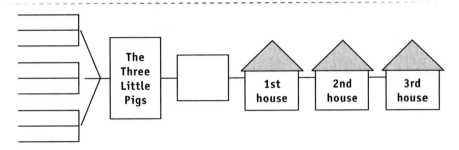

The teacher should think about the story in advance, determine what type of map best suits it, and then talk through it with the students. As is the case with the sample story map, it can be created to suit the particular story, rather than using a prepared or standard story map. Not only do story maps support student writing, but also their consistent use helps build comprehension and understanding of a story's necessary elements. Less advanced students can be provided with a list of the relevant vocabulary that they need to write the story. More advanced students can be directed to seek the words they need, thus providing more exposure to and review of the text.

Content-Area Big Books

An option for a post-unit activity is to create a group big book. The teacher should provide the overall structure of the book, which might be arranged by subtopics or responses to key topic questions. Another possibility is to create an alphabet book that consists of relevant words or phrases taken from the unit of study (as discussed in the "Beginning Writers" section). Students can sketch out large pictures, graphs, or other pictorial representations to illustrate the big book. Another possibility is to make enlarged photocopies of pictures taken from the student text or other sources, so that students can focus on writing rather than drawing.

Sentence Patterns

Informative/explanatory writing often contains patterns such as "because (of a fact or event), then (another fact)," "if … then …," and "when … then …." Pointing out these types of constructions in students' textbooks and discussing how information is organized increases students' comprehension. In addition, providing direct instruction and practice on these types of sentence patterns helps students develop the ability to use the patterns in their own writing (Peregoy and Boyle 2013).

Sentence Shortening

This process helps students create shorter sentences from lengthy and confusing ones (Peregoy and Boyle 2013). Sentence shortening can pertain to both narrative and informative/explanatory text. Using the basic subject–verb–object English sentence pattern is helpful for a teacher to point out to students as a model when they are learning to shorten sentences. The following are two examples of long sentences that should be arranged into shorter sentences.

That dog is the one that had puppies that the friends of their neighbors down the street bought and took home yesterday.

The solar system has nine planets that go in a circle around the sun called orbits and the closest ones to the sun are called the inner circle that have rocky surfaces so they are called terrestrial planets.

Structured Paragraphs

English language learners at the intermediate level should be introduced to, and experience repeated practice with, this standard paragraph format:

Topic sentence

Supporting sentence

Supporting sentence

Supporting sentence

Concluding sentence

Teachers should conduct an introductory discussion of this concept and provide students with several paragraphs that demonstrate the use of this structure. Subsequent lessons should include identifying paragraphs that follow this structure and some that do not follow this structure. Students should pinpoint the problems with paragraphs that do not follow this structure (e.g., the paragraph does not begin with a topic sentence, two sentences don't relate to the topic sentence, the concluding sentence doesn't summarize the main point, etc.). Students can also be presented with "scrambled sentences," or individually written sentences on strips of paper that need to be placed in the proper order: topic sentence, supporting details, and concluding sentence.

The next step is for students to write a paragraph to support a topic sentence. This could be done in small groups. Sample topic sentences should be prompts that address informative/explanatory and narrative subjects. Teachers should have students repeatedly practice one type until they demonstrate some level of proficiency, and then move on to practicing the other. Topic sentences should be taken from relevant thematic instruction. Structured paragraph writing is a useful scaffold for English learners. The following are starter suggestions for practice topic sentences:

- Protecting the environment is important.
- Being a member of a group helps animals survive.
- The best kind of pet to have is a ….
- Having a good friend is important for everyone.

What? So What? Now What?

The well-known and widely used know-want-learn (KWL) chart serves as the basis for this instructional strategy adaptation. The process takes many days to complete. Through discussion, the teacher and students identify a topic that the students are concerned with. The teacher creates a chart divided into three columns, labeling the columns with *What? So What?* and *Now What?* The *What?* column is the topic the students identify as problematic (e.g., "The playground is full of litter"). The group collectively brainstorms answers to the question *So What?* This segment can take many days to carefully think through and develop viable responses for. This is an excellent opportunity for students to state solutions and possibilities in their own terms and, with the teacher's guidance, to develop responses stated in academic language (e.g., "The playground is unsanitary," "It breeds harmful bugs," "It causes people to leave even more litter"). The students are then asked to propose possible solutions in the *Now What?* column (e.g., "We need to make a community awareness campaign," "We need to have a Clean Up Your School day"). This basic structure is a useful scaffold for helping students structure a form of logical and argumentative thinking and writing.

Advanced Writers

At this level of English language development, there is overlap between writing activities that support and benefit both advanced writers and fluent English students. Writing should include daily, short-term, focused writing tasks; provisional writing; writing to learn; on-demand writing to prompts; and writing to all three of the Common Core purposes. Students must also have opportunities to produce writing that is a result of extended writing tasks that include research, reflection, and revision (Evenson et al. 2013). The sections that follow provide suggestions that can supplement writing strategies the teacher may already use.

Figure 7.8 shows the text types and suggestions for associated activities for advanced writers.

Figure 7.8 Activities for Advanced Writers by Text Type

Text Type	Activities
Narrative	• Hotseating/reader response • Literature response journals
Informative/explanatory	• Compare and contrast • Double-entry journals • Surgical searches • Transitional words • Web quests
Argumentative	• Argumentative writing

Hotseating/Reader Response

This instructional tool works especially well with older students. The whole class or group reads the same piece of literature. Then, they write questions they would like to ask one of the characters. The students are arranged in small groups, and the teacher assigns one character to each group. The members of the small group become the experts on the assigned character. Each group prepares one individual to sit in the "hot seat" to answer questions from the whole group. The students then write a reflection about a particular character or story line and make connections to their own lives and circumstances. This type of close analysis of one character helps students develop depth in creating engaging characters in their own writing.

Literature Response Journals

Even students at the advanced level may find it difficult to respond to a piece of literature in completely unstructured ways. A modification is to organize students into groups so that each student has a specific responsibility or role. Role examples are word hunter, event analyzer, character analyzer, connector, and questioner. For each chapter in the book, the students maintain their responsibilities. The word hunter brings definitions for a predetermined number of words the group might have found difficult—no more than ten. The event analyzer searches for the key event(s) that occurred in the chapter. The character analyzer focuses on the important things about the character(s). The connector works on making a connection in some way to the students' lives. The questioner brings up important questions about this chapter. The students keep literature logs as they read and share with each other. This organization assigns focus and responsibility, and it provides opportunities for student discussion. Teachers who have consistently implemented this strategy throughout the duration of one chapter book have reported that it is an effective instructional tool with English learners, noting that students hold each other accountable for their responsibilities. The consistent use of literature response journals improves comprehension and the ability to write reflectively about the book.

Compare and Contrast

The verbs *compare* and *contrast* are the two most commonly used throughout the Common Core State Standards. It is important to give students ample opportunities to write questions that use these verbs. Students may rush into comparison before they have considered characteristics of individual entities first. One approach to helping students think about comparing and contrasting is to have them keep track of information as they are reading. For example, the teacher may ask students to keep track of the characteristics of types of clouds as the class is reading and discussing. Once they have recorded the individual qualities, characteristics, or attributes of each entity, they are then ready to contrast them. As a refinement, or an intermediary step between listing attributes and comparing them, students might be asked to rank the most important characteristics. This helps students use the most salient elements for comparison (e.g., "Cumulus clouds have clear edges"), as opposed to ones that may be of little significance (e.g., "Some clouds look white and some do not"). A top hat graphic organizer (the name comes from its resemblance to the outline of a top hat) can guide students and help them gather information in support of writing a compare/contrast analysis (Silver, Dewing, and Perini 2012). Compare/contrast writing is also the ideal time to promote the use of transition words (e.g., *in contrast*, *while*, *although*, *in comparison*).

Figure 7.9 shows a top hat graphic organizer with information about golden retrievers and Labrador retrievers and a compare/contrast paragraph. The left and right columns include specific information about each breed. In the "brim" of the top hat is a compare/contrast paragraph composed from the left and right columns about each breed of dog.

Figure 7.9 Comparing and Contrasting Labrador Retrievers and Golden Retrievers

Labrador Retrievers	Golden Retrievers
From Newfoundland; bred to help fishermen haul in nets; efficient game retrievers; family-friendly and affectionate; stable temperament; double-coated short hair, shed two times a year; short, straight hair that doesn't need lots of grooming; broad, flat tail and webbed feet make them good swimmers; tend to be explorers, which can make them independent and sometimes hard to train.	Bred in the Scottish Highlands to suit the climate and terrain; loving and loveable family dogs; eager to please; love to be around people; very calm and easy to train; double-coated long bushy coat that needs combing and regular grooming; shed twice a year; bushy tails and webbed feet make them excellent swimmers.

Labrador retrievers and golden retrievers are both friendly and affectionate dogs with stable temperaments. These qualities make both breeds excellent family dogs. Both breeds are hunting dogs, or retrievers, but they originated from different countries. Labs originated in Newfoundland and were originally bred to help fishermen haul in nets and catch fish that slipped through the nets. Goldens were originally bred in the Scottish Highlands to suit the Scottish terrain and weather. Both breeds are excellent swimmers and have webbed feet to help them swim. The golden retriever's bushy tail helps in swimming. In contrast, the Labrador retriever's broad, flat tail helps this breed swim. Although both breeds shed two times a year, Labs have short coats that make grooming easy. Goldens have longer coats that require careful grooming. While golden retrievers just love to be around people, Labrador retrievers tend to be explorers, so they can be harder to train.

Double-Entry Journals

Both the left and right sides of the brain are involved in processing information with double-entry journals. Before reading the relevant material, students first brainstorm on the left side of the page, asking questions and writing what they know or drawing pictures about the topic. The idea is to generate interest and activate prior knowledge that the students may have. Immediately after instruction and reading, students write down what they remember from the lesson.

Surgical Searches

The Common Core State Standards require students from the fourth grade to locate appropriate sources for research and draw detailed information and evidence from these to support their ideas in writing (CCSSO 2010). Surgical searches engage students in skimming large portions of text and extracting just the most relevant and necessary information. This strategy teaches and gives practice to students in sourcing useful information by using key words and phrases in large blocks of online text (Dappolone 2013). They practice extracting specific information for quick classroom-based conversation and reference. This activity also helps students locate possible sources for later use, in writing for more extended purposes.

Transition Words

In addition to practice with the structured paragraphs described previously, English learners need to learn to expand their writing into longer discourse. Figure 7.10 presents a list of transitional words that can be used as springboards into longer pieces of writing. Repeated practice with just a few of these phrases at a time improves students' confidence and their ability to incorporate the words into their writing.

Figure 7.10 Transition Words

Time/Sequence	Compare/Contrast	Summary	Direction
first of all	equally important	to sum up	on the opposite side
in the first place	by comparison	to summarize	close to
secondly	in comparison to	in summary	underneath
once	to compare	in brief	above
then	equally	in short	between
now	on the other hand	as has been noted	across from
meanwhile	by contrast	in conclusion	farther
while	unfortunately	to conclude	nearby
soon		as I have stated	
soon after		in other words	
after			
in the meantime			
later			
further			
next			
finally			
afterward			
at the same time			
Connecting	**Conditional**	**Cause/Effect**	
in spite of	even though	as a result	
in addition	unless	therefore	
again		for this reason	
besides		consequently	
		accordingly	

Web Quests

As discussed in Chapter 6, a web quest is an inquiry-based learning format in which the information that students seek and read comes from the Internet. Students conduct research on a "quest" set out for them. The sources are preselected by the teacher (or the designer of the web quest) so that students do not spend time looking for information sources, but rather seek information from the sources. Web quests require students to read, make choices and decisions about selecting the necessary information, and synthesize their newly gained knowledge in coherent ways, giving them ownership of the content they are writing about. Web quests promote collaborative thinking, reading, discussing, and writing. They guide students in using the Internet for research, in engaging them in thinking, and in developing research skills necessary in today's world.

Argument Writing

While persuasive writing appeals to emotion, argument writing requires students to appeal to logic and provide factual support (Evenson et al. 2013). Argument writing is the essence of the Common Core Anchor Standard for Writing 1: "Write arguments to support claims in an analysis of substantive topics or texts using valid reasoning and relevant and sufficient evidence" (CCSSO 2010, 18). This type of writing is a challenge for English learners and young writers, so reading and discussing several examples of both persuasive and argumentative writing is an important first step in helping them understand the difference. Helping students incorporate facts and numbers—anything quantifiable, verifiable, and reliably sourced—is the key. A repeated cycle of researching, orally debating, and then writing about the information helps students grasp the thinking that supports writing in this way. The following are suggested topics for prompting oral debate that serves as a scaffold for written discourse:

- Cell phones should not be allowed on school property.
- Students should receive rewards for earning good grades.
- Violence in video games is harmful.
- Zoos are jails for animals.

Summary

Writing clearly and accurately is a challenging task that English language learners face. This is because writing requires students to produce language in ways that combine many aspects of language: using descriptive language and creativity in developing engaging narrative; having a clear grasp of grammar and syntax; expressing oneself in a logical, step-by-step progression; incorporating new vocabulary based on new knowledge; and writing academic language that is structured and formal, and very different from everyday language used outside the classroom. Finally, clear and accurate writing means that students must demonstrate thinking and reasoning skills, and apply these to suit the purpose, audience, and task of the writing assignment.

While underlying principles apply to all writers, this chapter discussed specific types of support for English learners. These include using patterns, models, and organizational techniques that help scaffold writing; providing extra vocabulary support; offering collaborative writing opportunities; and giving specific writing feedback. Teachers should accustom English language learners to on-demand writing, and they can encourage students to use oral language and their primary language to support developing writing abilities in English. In addition, teachers should provide English learners with opportunities to write to the requirements of the Common Core, taking into consideration their linguistic developmental level.

Apply, Reflect, and Extend

1. Do your students require more assistance in writing narrative or informative/explanatory text? Why do you think this is true? Which strategies might be most useful in helping them develop into better all-around writers?

2. In what ways do your students support their own learning through writing? How might you extend these opportunities?

3. What writing opportunities do your students have on a regular basis? How much time in a week do they spend writing? Roughly what percentage of time is devoted to writing narratives and informative/explanatory text? Given some of the options presented in this chapter, in what ways can you expand your students' writing time?

4. Which vocabulary strategies from Chapter 5 might you incorporate with the writing strategies discussed in this chapter to improve your students' writing?

Chapter 8

Thinking through and Organizing for Instruction

Anticipatory Quiz

Are the following statements true or false?

_____ **1.** Standards and curriculum are distinct entities.

_____ **2.** Assessment should be embedded in curriculum design.

_____ **3.** The Common Core State Standards provide curriculum sources.

_____ **4.** "Big ideas" or enduring understandings are difficult for English learners to grasp.

_____ **5.** Long-term research projects are out of reach language-wise for English learners.

"Begin with the end in mind."

—Stephen Covey

In *Understanding by Design* (2005), Grant Wiggins and Jay McTighe guide teachers to think "backward" through the teaching and learning processes. The four fundamental questions that they pose in backward planning are as follows:

1. What learning outcomes are expected of students? What should students know and be able to do?

2. What are indicators of learning success? What do students need to do to demonstrate understanding?

3. How will these be assessed?

4. What learning experiences will students need to get them there?

The title of the College and Career Readiness (CCR) Anchor Standards address the first point: students are expected to be college and career ready (CCSSO 2010). In recent work focused on the Common Core State Standards, Wiggins and McTighe distinguish between standards and curriculum. While the Common Core states clear outcomes, they place the development of the learning experiences in the hands of educators. They call for teachers to "translate the Standards into an engaging and effective curriculum" (McTighe and Wiggins 2013, 27). Developing meaningful curriculum helps students achieve the stated outcomes.

In *Understanding by Design*, the authors lay out a second framework that guides teachers in making such curricular decisions and plans. The four framing questions they pose concerning curriculum development are as follows:

1. To what extent does the idea, topic, or process represent a "big idea" that has enduring value beyond the classroom?

2. To what extent does the idea, topic, or process reside at the heart of the discipline?

3. To what extent does the idea, topic, or process present conceptual difficulties or harbor misconceptions and, therefore, require studying to promote understanding?

4. To what extent does the idea, topic, or process offer potential for engaging students? (Wiggins and McTighe 2005, 10–11)

Engaging students in curriculum that is designed with these four points as the basis helps ensure that they will practice and develop the abilities required by the Common Core. Such curriculum affords students the opportunities to

- improve their overall English language skills;
- improve their ability to speak and write in a clear and cogent manner;
- learn to read with understanding; and
- analyze, question, think critically, and engage in problem solving.

What, then, are the types of support that English learners need for curriculum access and for improving English language abilities? What are particular planning considerations for teachers? In contrast to previous chapters that focused on specific teaching strategies, this chapter offers a longer view: thinking through and planning for instruction that provides curriculum access and rich English language learning opportunities.

Essential Elements in Planning Instruction for English Learners

As discussed in previous chapters, students are best served by teachers who

- make ideas concrete and discernible;
- link language and vocabulary to concepts so that once those are understood, students begin to build their use of language around them; and
- provide models and structures to help scaffold understanding and language use.

In addition, and more specifically, planning should include

- developing specific and distinct content and language objectives;
- offering sufficient oral discussion and multiple passes of the relevant material in order to build background knowledge and comprehension;

- ensuring multiple opportunities to reinforce understanding and learning through listening, speaking, reading, and writing;

- organizing meaningful peer interaction based on productive academic tasks;

- providing clear and direct feedback;

- developing opportunities for students to make personal connections with key concepts; and

- assessing in ways that permit students to demonstrate understanding commensurate with their language abilities, and that do not necessarily rely exclusively on written or spoken English.

In thinking through and organizing for instruction, teachers may find the type of framework shown in Figure 8.1 helpful. It lays out the key components for thematic unit planning and contains the elements for designing instruction for students who are English learners and fluent English speakers. Both types of students are considered and planned for, reflecting the teaching reality of many educators. Please refer to Appendix D for a full-size version of the framework.

Figure 8.1 Thematic Unit Organizational Framework

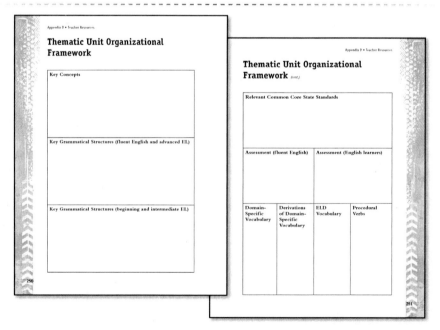

Thinking through and Organizing for Instruction: A Sample Thematic Unit

The following example shows how a teacher might think through and plan for a thematic unit. It looks at the teacher's thinking process and basic planning, and lays out two sample lessons. The sample lessons demonstrate how teachers can use and adapt just a few of the strategies discussed in previous chapters.

Here are the teacher's overall goals:

- **Goal 1:** Use content instruction that helps students develop the necessary skills to meet Common Core requirements in English language arts and history/social studies for grades 6–8.

- **Goal 2:** Develop an overall framework and daily lessons.

- **Goal 3:** Provide instruction that addresses the learning needs of English learners and fluent English speakers in the classroom.

Here again are Wiggins and McTighe's (2005) four framing questions for developing curriculum and the application of the questions to this teacher's thematic unit:

1. To what extent does the idea, topic, or process represent a "big idea" that has enduring value beyond the classroom?

   The teacher decides upon a question that has enduring value beyond the classroom: What makes a civilization? Related questions are as follows: What makes a civilization great? Are some civilizations not as great as others? How does one determine this? What makes a civilization endure or crumble? Students will be asked to think about these ideas throughout their academic experiences. Examining a great ancient civilization, Ancient Egypt, may give them ways to start thinking about and comparing contemporary societies to each other and to those that previously existed. Students can reflect on these enduring questions for some time to come.

2. To what extent does the idea, topic, or process reside at the heart of the discipline?

   The questions posed previously relate to the discipline of history.

3. To what extent does the idea, topic, or process present conceptual difficulties or harbor misconceptions and therefore require studying to promote understanding?

Students may have some general ideas about mummies or pyramids that they associate with Egypt; however, these ideas may be inaccurate or limited in scope. Students may not understand that every great civilization is based on necessary and fundamental societal structures and developments.

4. To what extent does the idea, topic, or process offer potential for engaging students?

Innumerable ways exist to get students hooked on finding something fascinating about this ancient civilization. The intent of this thematic unit is to develop students' depth of understanding, rather than promoting an all-encompassing breadth of knowledge about ancient Egypt, or requiring students to merely memorize facts and figures. The lessons are designed to engage students in thinking processes and ways of using and expanding reasoning, as well as develop and apply listening, speaking, reading, and writing abilities. The lessons build upon each other and help students develop an understanding of the fundamental question: What makes a civilization?

Here again are Wiggins and McTighe's (2005) four questions concerning backward planning and the application of the questions to this teacher's thematic unit:

1. What learning outcomes are expected of students? What should students know and be able to do?

The learning outcomes are shown in Figure 8.2 under Key Concepts. What students should know and be able to do is addressed in the content and language objectives for each lesson.

2. What are indicators of learning success? What do students need to do to demonstrate understanding?

There are required demonstrations of understanding throughout the thematic unit in daily discussion, class participation, assignments, and homework.

The students will also conduct a long-term research project. In pairs, students identify an area of interest and carry out a research project for which they will produce a process or product that exemplifies and elucidates an aspect of ancient Egypt. A few examples are as follows:

- Examine why and how a particular tool or armament was developed and made.

- Describe the natural products and processes used to develop skin care and makeup that both men and women used.

- Describe a particular craftsperson's process, such as the lost wax method of making a gold object.

As a group, beginning and intermediate English learners will carry out their research project with the teacher's support and guidance. They will research, discuss, and write about the ancient Egyptians' ability to measure time. They will demonstrate how Egyptians measured time by making a shadow clock and a water clock. The teacher decided to study time measurement with English learners because the concept is tangible and concrete enough to provide comprehensible input. The concrete nature of time measurement provides a learning scaffold. At the same time, the topic permits students to explore, research, understand, and explain an important technology developed by the ancient Egyptians.

One of the most important aspects of the project is for all students to respond to the following questions:

- What does this tell us about ancient Egypt?

- What was the significance of this to the Egyptians?

All students will present their research to class members as one of the thematic unit's culminating experiences. In preparation, students will carefully identify their idea, discuss it with the teacher at its various stages of development, conduct long-term research, synthesize information from a variety of sources, collaborate with a partner, and make a clear and thoughtful oral presentation about it to their fellow students. These processes reflect Common Core requirements that students must demonstrate.

3. How will these (indicators of learning success) be assessed?

The teacher should establish points and a grading system on all assignments and discuss the major assignments with students. The teacher and students should examine the relevant samples of student writing in Appendix C of the CCSS to help them understand what they should strive for in their writing.

4. What learning experiences will students need to get them there?

Examples are as follows:

- Conduct a pre-assessment of students' knowledge of important ideas about ancient Egypt.
- Run/walk 1 mile and make mathematic calculations of the required time to navigate the Nile River.
- Observe and participate in a map re-creation of the Nile River.
- Expand word use and word knowledge by using affixes with key vocabulary.
- Write compare/contrast descriptions of homes and clothing of humble and wealthy families.
- Participate in a gallery walk to create class information charts about ancient Egypt.
- Participate in a visual language experience approach and write about the experience.
- Use a "listen first, talk later" strategy of comparing notes in pairs and in groups of four.

Note that the following is an example of how a teacher might create a thematic unit organizational framework. Specific key concepts, grammatical structures, vocabulary, assessments, relevant Common Core State Standards, and learning experiences are merely suggestions for how a teacher might approach such planning. The thematic unit organizational framework will vary from teacher to teacher and should be developed around students' learning needs. A template for the thematic unit organizational framework is found in Appendix D.

Key Concepts

- The Nile River served as a vital resource that supported transportation and agricultural development.

- The Egyptians built an economic surplus based on the Nile River's resources.

- Economic strength contributed to Egypt's political and cultural power.

- Rulers extended ancient Egypt's trade, wealth, and power.

- The Egyptians developed a complex society of social classes, roles, and responsibilities.

- The Egyptians made many advances in geometry, medicine, agriculture, and astronomy.

- The Egyptians developed many systems: a writing system, a counting system, a linear measuring system, systems to measure time, and a religious structure.

- The ancient Egyptians developed fine arts and practical crafts that supported their lives.

- Ancient Egypt was a strong and unified civilization that maintained religious, social, and political order for nearly 3,000 years.

Key Grammatical Structures

Fluent English and advanced English learners:

Instruction and practice writing:

- Compare/contrast responses using compare/contrast transition words: *however, in contrast, on the one hand, on the other hand, as opposed to, equally important, by comparison, in comparison to, to compare, equally, by contrast, unfortunately*

- Informative/explanatory text sequence patterns: *because of* (a fact or event), *if ... then ..., when ... then ...*

Key Grammatical Structures

Beginning and intermediate English learners:

- past tense *-ed*
- present progressive *-ing*
- prepositional phrases (*in the*, *along the*, *next to*, *beside*)

Relevant Common Core State Standards

- CCSS.ELA-Literacy.RH.6-8.7: Integrate visual information (e.g., in charts, graphs, photographs, videos, or maps) with other information in print and digital texts.

- CCSS.ELA-Literacy.CCRA.R.7: Integrate and evaluate content presented in diverse media and formats, including visually and quantitatively, as well as in words.

- CCSS.ELA-Literacy.CCRA.L.6: Acquire and use accurately a range of general academic and domain-specific words and phrases; demonstrate independence in gathering vocabulary knowledge when encountering an unknown term important to comprehension or expression.

- CCSS.ELA-Literacy.CCRA.W.7: Conduct short as well as more sustained research projects based on focused questions.

- CCSS.ELA-Literacy.CCRA.W.10: Write routinely over extended time frames and shorter time frames for a range of tasks, purposes, and audiences.

Assessment	
Fluent English and Advanced English Learners:	**Beginning and Intermediate English Learners:**
Make daily entries in a personal social studies journal of new words; add new concepts.	Make daily entries in a personal social studies journal of new words; add a concept and/or sketch of at least one new idea.
Participate actively in a gallery walk.	Participate actively in a gallery walk.
Provide in-class responses to the introductory lesson "What did you discover?" assignment.	Write at least five phrases or sentences to describe a person or a home of a wealthy family or a humble family.
Write a compare/contrast paper on wealthy versus humble homes and manner of dress.	Participate actively in the Rosetta Stone in-class activity.
Participate actively in the Rosetta Stone in-class activity.	Provide feedback and assessment at determined stages of the culminating research project.
Provide feedback and assessment at determined stages of the culminating research project.	Create a found poem from a previously unseen text.
Create a found poem from a previously unseen text.	Actively participate in creating an ABC concept book about important aspects of ancient Egypt.
Write an essay on the topic "What makes a civilization?"	Actively participate in group research and presentation of the research project.
Actively participate in research and presentation of the research project.	

Domain-Specific Vocabulary* (fluent English and advanced EL)	Derivations of Domain-Specific Vocabulary	ELD Vocabulary (beginning and intermediate)	Procedural Verbs
resource	resourcefulness, source, sourced	to explain	to cite
isolate	isolation, isolated	to barter	to compare
inhospitable	hospitable, hospital, hospitalization	details	to contrast
society	fertilize, fertilizer	gift	to determine
ruler	nutrition, nutritional	resource	to distinguish
merchant	precision, imprecise, precisely	humble	to incorporate
craftsman	scribble, inscribed, scripture	wealthy	to infer
delta	supporting, unsupported	riches	to locate
silt	civilized, civil, uncivil, civility, incivility	delta	to support
fertile	enormity	society	
nutrients	to advance, advanced	technologies	
precise	en- (entomb, encase)	precise	
scribes		(Beginning EL)	
Rosetta Stone		prepositions: on, along	
civilization		nouns: fish, crops, animals, soil	
enormous		verbs: building, sorting, plowing, fishing, loading	
advancements			

* Bold words indicate English learner vocabulary students should strive to learn.

Sample Lesson 1

Content Objective: Students will express the reasoning behind the statement that the Nile River was called a gift.

Language Objective: Students will use key vocabulary in speaking or writing: *resource, inhospitable, isolated.*

(The Nile River was a rich <u>resource</u>. The regions beyond the Nile River were <u>inhospitable</u> deserts. The desert regions to the east and to the west of the great river <u>isolated</u> the people who lived along it.)

Activity: Introductory discussion and provisional writing

CCSS Connections:

- CCSS.ELA-Literacy.RH.6–8.7: Integrate visual information (e.g., in charts, graphs, photographs, videos, or maps) with other information in print and digital texts.

- CCSS.ELA-Literacy.CCRA.R.7: Integrate and evaluate content presented in diverse media and formats, including visually and quantitatively, as well as in words.

Other Lesson Requirements: Hold brief paired conversation, use inferential thinking, use multiple resources to support learning, and use brief provisional writing to support learning.

Lesson:

All students are together. The teacher shows students a beautifully wrapped gift. Can they guess what is inside? Hint: "Long ago and far away." Inside are a gold pin of the sphinx, a gold ring from Egypt with embedded semiprecious native stones, a miniature pyramid, and a picture of Nefertiti painted on papyrus. Each item is a visual representation of an important aspect of ancient Egypt. The teacher briefly explains what each item represents.

Students discuss with each other in pairs for about four minutes each: "What do you know about Egypt?" The teacher hands out paper. When the teacher says "Egypt," students write what comes to mind. Students should write everything they can in the allotted amount of time. Beginning and intermediate English learners may sketch and add phrases. This serves as a pre-assessment for both the teacher and students.

The class watches two video clips that introduce the basics of ancient Egypt and life along the Nile River. They initially watch with no sound to focus on the visuals, and then once more with volume.

Fluent English and advanced-level students may review the video clips. They skim the relevant section in their social studies text about ancient Egypt. They may explore the library books that the teacher has made available. They respond in writing to the following assignment.

While fluent English and advanced-level English students work, the teacher conducts a preview lesson of the thematic unit to beginning and intermediate students, who have also viewed the videos. The visuals have likely helped them develop some degree of background knowledge.

What Did You Discover?

Drawing your information from videos, the library books, and your textbook, respond to the following:

1. Justify the reasoning that supports calling the Nile River a gift.

2. What were ancient Egyptians known for? What did they develop? There are many, many choices!

   - a.
   - b.
   - c.
   - d.

3. Based on the video clips you saw today, what lies beyond the Nile River to the east and to the west?

4. Using inferential thinking, what significance did the geography surrounding the Nile River have? Infer why this mattered. Hint: You may want to use the words *inhospitable* and *isolated* to help you think about answering this question.

The teacher has a second gift box. Can students guess what is inside? Inside are little figures or pictures: fish, wheat, cow, duck, goat, bucket, boat, and seeds—all concrete items. The teacher explains in short, direct sentences that these are gifts of the Nile River. This is what the river gave people or helped people with. The teacher acts out fishing from the river, pouring water for animals, pouring water on seeds, the boat sailing on the river, and men taking goods on and off the boat, all the while talking slowly and in short sentences or phrases about these acts for students to associate meaning with the words and activities. The teacher uses the word *agriculture* to indicate seeds, soil, water, crops, and growing. The teacher acts out bartering goods with a few of students. They record in their journals: "Gifts from the Nile River: fish, crops, water, animals, soil, agriculture, and barter." The students look through several library books that contain excellent illustrations for vocabulary and concept reinforcement. The teacher encourages students to comment and ask questions about what they see, and with help, they write these comments and questions in their journals. With some help, and using the library books as resources, students complete the following vocabulary activity by writing in or placing a check in the appropriate box.

	Here is what this word or phrase means: (in my language) (in a drawing) (in a phrase in English)	I have seen this word or phrase and it might mean something like…	I have seen this word or phrase but I'm not sure what it means.	I really can't figure out what this word/ phrase means.
barter Egyptians bartered agricultural goods with other people.				
agriculture The Nile River helped the people develop agriculture.				
natural resources Egyptians had many natural resources, like good soil, water, and fish and animals for food.				
strong civilization The Nile River helped Egypt develop into a strong civilization.				

Closure:

The whole class reconvenes. In pairs, each student shares four facts he or she learned and one thing he or she is curious about and would like to find out. Each pair shares one fact and one question with the class.

Sample Lesson 2

Content Objective: Students will express orally or in writing the significance of the development of hieroglyphics, and in writing the significance of the Rosetta Stone.

Language Objective: Students will use the following patterns in writing:

because of (a fact or event), *if … then …,* and *when … then …*

Students will include at least three transition words in their writing: *however, in contrast, on the one hand, on the other hand, equally important, equally, by contrast, unfortunately*

Vocabulary: *hieroglyphics, papyrus, scribes, Rosetta Stone*

Activity: Developing depth of understanding of vocabulary and the concepts they represent

CCSS Connections:

- CCSS.ELA-Literacy.CCRA.L.6: Acquire and use accurately a range of general academic and domain-specific words and phrases; demonstrate independence in gathering vocabulary knowledge when encountering an unknown term important to comprehension or expression.

- CCSS.ELA-Literacy.CCRA.W.7: Conduct short as well as more sustained research projects based on focused questions.

- CCSS.ELA-Literacy.CCRA.W.10: Write routinely over extended time frames and shorter time frames for a range of tasks, purposes, and audiences.

Other Lesson Requirements: Skim for information, use contextual clues to discern meaning, and engage in an academic conversation.

Lesson:

All students are together. Beginning-level English learners may not comprehend everything; however, all students will be seeking to enrich their understanding of the lesson's key vocabulary and concepts, and jotting down phrases and pictures of them. The key vocabulary and concepts will also be discussed in a whole group with supporting pictures and video clips.

Assign a key vocabulary word to each pair. The students fold a piece of paper in fourths. They complete 1, 2, and 3 (see the following example). Then, students skim their textbooks and look in library books to expand their understanding of their assigned word, completing the fourth quadrant only when they are certain of the meaning.

1. Word	**2.** Word used in a sentence
3. What the student thinks it means	**4.** Depiction and definition of the word's meaning

On a second sheet of paper, each pair writes the definition of their word and makes a sketch to depict its meaning. These are posted on the front board according to word category. Each pair may comment on their word's meaning and sketch. The teacher adds to students' definitions and gives a deeper explanation of each word and its importance in the context of ancient Egypt and beyond. Students view a video clip or two about hieroglyphics, the role of scribes, the making of papyrus, and the discovery of the Rosetta Stone. They hold a class discussion guided by the teacher.

hieroglyphics	papyrus	scribes	Rosetta Stone
(Students place their papers here in the correct column.)			

Questions for Class Discussion:

- Do hieroglyphics consist of sounds like an alphabet or symbols that carry meaning? Are there hieroglyphics on tombs? Where do you see hieroglyphics?

- Should making papyrus be considered technology? What would make it a technology? Are the special brushes and the paints the Egyptians developed technologies? Why/why not?

- What did scribes write? Who was the audience, and why and what were they writing? Does every writer have to consider task, audience, and purpose? As a writer, do *you* have to consider task, audience, and purpose?

- Why was the Rosetta Stone such an important discovery? In what ways is biliteracy useful?

Learning Center Option:

The teacher may organize a learning center where students can practice developing their own secret code and making their own "Rosetta Stone." This is an excellent opportunity to have students who write languages other than English make translations of the codes into their own languages. So, for example, a Rosetta Stone may be the student's invented and coded message, the same message written in English, and the message written in a language that a student in the class can write. Creating language codes promotes logic and critical thinking. Many websites offer information on helping students learn to develop secret codes.

Closure:

To conclude the class discussion on the four key vocabulary words, the teacher asks student pairs to write a one-page summary about the meaning of the word of their choice, and add points of interest they learned during the class discussion. The teacher may work with the group of English learners to accomplish this assignment, or students may be paired with fluent English students. Students will include transition words such as *because of... if... then...* and *when... then...* in the assignment.

Summary

In considering curriculum development, the concept of backward planning provided by Wiggins and McTighe's work offers an excellent framework for teachers. Using a thematic unit organizational framework as suggested in this chapter helps teachers plan for and implement essential instructional elements that address learning needs for English learners and fluent English speakers alike. This type of planning framework not only helps ensure that students develop increased language facility, but also helps ensure access to the kinds of mental processing and critical thinking that students must develop in order to achieve academic success.

Apply, Reflect, and Extend

Using Wiggins and McTighe's framework for curriculum development, identify a topic for a thematic unit.

1. Based on the thematic unit, address the framework's four key questions.

2. Identify Internet resources and other supplementary material such as library books to develop teaching ideas and to provide student learning support.

3. Establish content objectives and language objectives. Base objectives and outcomes on the CCSS. Identify which standards you will address.

4. Select focus vocabulary for English learners and fluent English speakers.

5. Develop student activities and aligned assessments that ensure student understanding as well as provide opportunities to foster critical thinking.

References Cited

Achieve, Inc. 2013. *Next Generation Science Standards*. http://www.
nextgenscience.org/next-generation-science-standards, accessed April
5, 2014.

Ardasheva, Yuliya, Sze Sze Tong, and Thomas Tretter. 2012. "Validating the
English Language Learner Motivation Scale: Pre-College to Measure Language
Learning Motivational Orientations Among Young ELLS." *Learning and
Individual Differences* 22: 473–483.

August, Diane, Maria Carlo, Cheryl Dressler, and Catherine Snow. 2005. "The
Critical Role of Vocabulary Development for English Learners." *Learning
Disabilities Research and Practice* 20 (1): 50–57.

August, Diane, and Timothy Shanahan. 2006. *Developing Literacy in Second-Language
Learners: Report of the National Literacy Panel on Language-Minority Children and
Youth*. Mahwah, NJ: Lawrence Erlbaum Associates.

Austin, John L. 1976. *How to Do Things with Words*, 2nd ed. Oxford, UK: Oxford
University Press.

Bear, Donald, Marcia Invernizzi, Shane Templeton, and Francine Johnston. 2012.
Words Their Way, 5th ed. Boston: Pearson.

Beck, Isabel, Margaret McKeown, and Linda Kucan. 2002. Bringing Words to Life:
Robust Vocabulary Instruction. New York: The Guilford Press.

Beck, Isabel, Margaret G. McKeown, and Linda Kucan. 2008. *Creating Robust
Vocabulary: Frequently Asked Questions and Extended Examples*. New York: Guilford.

Biemiller, Andrew. 2003. "Oral Comprehension Sets the Ceiling on Reading
Comprehension." *American Educator* 27 (1).

Blachowicz, Camille L. Z., and Connie Obrochta. 2005. "Vocabulary Visits:
Virtual Field Trips for Content Vocabulary Development." *The Reading Teacher*
59 (3): 262–268.

Boerman-Cornell, Bill. 2013. "More Than Comic Books." *Educational Leadership*
70 (6): 73–77.

Bowers, Erica, and Laura Keisler. 2011. *Building Academic Language Through
Content-Area Text*. Huntington Beach, CA: Shell Education.

Brechtel, Marcia. 2001. *Bringing It All Together*. Carlsbad, CA: Dominie.

Browne, Charles, Brent Culligan, and Joseph Phillips. 2013. New General Service List. Accessed September 25, 2013, www.newgeneralservicelist.org.

Bruner, Jerome. 1974. *Toward a Theory of Instruction*. Cambridge, MA: Harvard University Press.

Chomsky, Noam. 1965. *Aspects of the Theory of Syntax*. Cambridge, MA: MIT Press.

———. 1968. *Language and Mind*. New York: Harcourt, Brace, & World.

Content Standards. 2012. *English Language Development Content Standards*. Sacramento, CA: California Department of Education.

Content Standards. 2011. *English Language Proficiency Standards*. Topeka, KS: Kansas State Department of Education.

Content Standards. 2012. *Languages Other than English (LOTE) Texas Essential Knowledge and Skills*. Austin, TX: Texas Education Agency.

Coxhead, Averil. 2000. "A New Academic Word List." *TESOL Quarterly* 34 (2): 213—238.

———. 2011. "The Academic Word List 10 Years On: Research and Teaching Implications." *TESOL Quarterly* 45 (2): 355–362.

Cummins, James. 1981. "The Role of Primary Language Development in Promoting Educational Success for Language Minority Students." In *Schooling and Language Minority Students: A Theoretical Framework*, edited by California State Department of Education, 3–49. Los Angeles: Evaluation, Dissemination and Assessment Center, California State University.

———. 2000. *Language, Power, and Pedagogy: Bilingual Children in the Crossfire*. Clevedon, England: Multilingual Matters.

Cunningham, Anne E., Jamie Zibulsky, Keith E. Stanovich, and Paula J. Stanovich. 2009. "How Teachers Would Spend Their Time Teaching Language Arts: The Mismatch Between Self-Reported and Best Practice." *Journal of Learning Disabilities* 42 (5): 418–430.

Dappolone, Michael. 2013. "Making Best Practice Better." *Educational Leadership* 70 (6): 69–72.

Daskalovska, Nina, Lijana Koleva Gudeva, and Bijana Ivanovska. 2012. "Learner Motivation and Interest." *Procedia—Social and Behavioral Sciences* 46: 1187–1191.

Deacon, S. Hélène, Lesly Wade-Woolley, and John Kirby. 2007. "Crossover: The Role of Morphological Awareness in French Immersion Children's Reading." *Developmental Psychology* 43: 732.

Dressler, Cheryl, Maria S. Carlo, Catherine E. Snow, Diane August, and Claire E. White. 2011. "Spanish-Speaking Students' Use of Cognate Knowledge to Infer Meaning of English Words." *Bilingualism, Language and Cognition* 14 (2): 243–255.

Dutro, Susana, and Ellen Levy. 2012. "Equipping Adolescent English Learners for Academic Achievement: An Interview with Susana Dutro and Ellen Levy." *Journal of Adolescent & Adult Literacy* 55 (4): 339–342.

Echevarría, Jana J., and Anne Graves. 2011. *Sheltered Content Instruction*. Boston: Allyn and Bacon.

Echevarría, Jana J., MaryEllen Vogt, and Deborah J. Short. 2012. *Making Content Comprehensible for English Learners: The SIOP Model*, 4th ed. Boston: Pearson.

ELP Standards. 2007. *World-Class Instructional Design and Assessment (WIDA)*. Madison, WI: Board of Regents of the University of Wisconsin System.

Evenson, Amber, Monette McIver, Susan Ryan, and Amitra Schwols. 2013. *Common Core Standards: For Elementary Grades 3–5 Math and English Language Arts*. Alexandria, VA: ASCD.

Goldenberg, Claude. 2008. "Teaching English Language Learners: What the Research Does—and Does Not—Say." *American Educator* 32 (2): 8–23 and 42–44.

Graddol, David. 2006. "English Next: Why Global English May Mean the End of 'English as a Foreign Language'." The British Council. Accessed July 5, 2013, www.britishcouncil.org/learning-research-english-next.pdf.

Graves, Michael F. 1987. "Roles of Instruction in Fostering Vocabulary Development." In *The Nature of Vocabulary Acquisition*, edited by Margaret G. McKeown and Mary E. Curtis, 165–184. Hillsdale, NJ: Erlbaum.

Grice, Paul. 1975. "Logic and Conversation." In *Syntax and Semantics, Volume 3: Speech Acts*, edited by Peter Cole and Jerry L. Morgan, 41–58. New York, NY: Academic Press.

Gunderson, Lee. 2009. *ESL (ELL) Literacy Instruction: A Guidebook to Theory and Practice*, 2nd ed. New York: Routledge.

Gunning, Thomas. 2013. *Creating Literacy Instruction for All Students*. 8th ed. Boston: Pearson.

Hadaway, Nancy L. 2009. "A Narrow Bridge to Academic Reading." *Educational Leadership* 66 (7): 38–41.

Helman, Lori, Donald Bear, Shane Templeton, Marci Invernizzi, and Francine Johnston. 2011. *Words Their Way With English Learners: Word Study*. Boston, Upper Saddle River, NJ: Pearson Merrill Prentice Hall.

Hirsch, E. D. 2003. "Reading Comprehension Requires Knowledge—of Words and the World." *American Educator* 27 (1): 10–29.

Hirsch, E. D., and Lisa Hansel. 2013. "Why Content Is King." *Educational Leadership* 71 (3): 28–33.

Kieffer, Michael J., and Nonie K. Lesaux. 2008. "The Role of Derivational Morphological Awareness in the Reading Comprehension of Spanish–Speaking English Language Learners." *Reading and Writing: An Interdisciplinary Journal* 21: 783–804.

———. 2012. "Direct and Indirect Roles of Morphological Awareness in the English Reading Comprehension of Native English, Spanish, Filipino, and Vietnamese Speakers." *Language Learning* 62 (4): 1170–1204.

Kist, William. 2013. "New Literacies and the Common Core." *Educational Leadership* 70 (6): 38–43.

Krashen, Stephen. 2004. "The Case for Narrow Reading." *Language Magazine* 3 (5): 17–19.

Krashen, Stephen, and Tracy Terrell. 1983. *The Natural Approach: Language Acquisition in the Classroom.* Oxford, England: Pergamon Press.

Kucan, Linda. 2012. "What is Most Important to Know About Vocabulary?" *Reading Teacher* 65 (6): 360–366.

Lamott, Anne. 1995. *Bird by Bird.* New York: First Anchor Books.

Lawrence, Joshua F., Claire White, and Catherine E. Snow. 2010. "The Words Students Need." *Educational Leadership* 68 (2): 23–26.

Leveled Texts for Science: Earth and Space Science. 2008. Huntington Beach, CA: Shell Education.

McTighe, Jay, and Grant Wiggins. 2013. "From Common Core Standards to Curriculum: Five Big Ideas." *New Hampshire Journal of Education*: 25–31.

Miller, George A. 1969. *The Psychology of Communication: Seven Essays.* Baltimore, MD: Penguin Books.

Miller, Jon, John Heilmann, Ann Nockerts, Aquiles Iglesias, Leah Fabiano, and David Francis. 2006. "Oral Language and Reading in Bilingual Children." *Learning Disabilities Research & Practice* (21) 1: 30–43.

Nagy, William, and Dianna Townsend. 2012. "Words as Tools: Learning Academic Vocabulary as Language Acquisition." *Reading Research Quarterly* 47 (1): 91–108.

Nation, I. S. P. 2001. *Learning Vocabulary in Another Language.* Cambridge: Cambridge University Press.

National Association for Language Development in the Curriculum. 2012. Accessed June 18, 2013, www.naldic.org.uk/research-and-information/eal-statistics/eal--pupils.

National Governors Association (NGA) Center for Best Practices and Council of Chief State School Officers (CCSSO). 2010. "Common Core State Standards: English Language Arts Standards." Washington, DC: National Governors Association Center for Best Practices, Council of Chief State School Officers. www.corestandards.org.

O'Malley, J. Michael, and Lorraine Valdez Pierce. 1996. *Authentic Assessment for English Language Learners.* New York: Addison-Wesley Publishing.

Olsen, Laurie. 2010. *Reparable Harm: Fulfilling the Unkept Promise of Educational Opportunity for California's Long Term English Learners.* Long Beach, CA: Californians Together.

Oroujlou, Nassar, and Majid Vahedi. 2011. "Motivation, Attitude, and Language Learning." *Procedia—Social and Behavioral Sciences* 29: 994–1000.

Peregoy, Susana, and Owen Boyle. 2013. *Reading, Writing, and Learning in ESL: A Resource Book for Teaching K–12 English Learners.* 6th ed. Boston: Pearson.

Piaget, Jean. 1969. *Psychology of the Child.* New York, NY: Basic Books.

———. 1990. *The Child's Conception of the World.* New York, NY: Littlefield Adams.

Pyle, Howard. 2013. "The Merry Adventures of Robin Hood," in *Leveled Text for Classic Fiction: Adventure*, edited by Debra J. Housel, 111. Huntington Beach, CA: Shell Education.

Ramirez, Gloria, Xi Chen, and Adrian Pasquarella. 2013. "Cross-Linguistic Transfer of Morphological Awareness in Spanish-Speaking English Language Learners." *Topics in Language Disorder* 33 (1): 73–92.

Rasinski, Tim, Nancy Padak, Rick Newton, and Evangeline Newton. 2008. *Greek and Latin Roots: Keys to Building Vocabulary.* Huntington Beach, CA: Shell Education.

Saiegh-Haddad, E., and Esther Geva. 2008. "Morphological Awareness, Phonological Awareness, and Reading in English-Arabic Bilingual Children." *Reading and Writing* 21: 481–504.

Saunders, William, and Claude Goldenberg. 2010. "Research to Guide English Language Development (ELD) Instruction." In *Improving Education for English Learners; Research-Based Approaches*, edited by California Department of Education. Sacramento, CA: CDE Press.

Schiff, Rachel, and Sharon Calif. 2007. "Role of Phonological and Morphological Awareness in L2 Oral Word Reading." *Language Learning* 57: 271–298.

Silver, Harvey, R. Thomas Dewing, and Matthew J. Perini. 2012. *The Core Six Essential Strategies for Achieving Excellence with the Common Core.* Alexandria, VA: ASCD.

Snow, Marguerite Ann, and Anne Katz. 2010. "English Language Development: Issues and Implementation at Grades K through 5." In California Department of Education (Ed.), *Improving Education for English Learners: Research-Based Approaches*, 83–148. Sacramento, CA: Department of Education.

Sprenger, Marilee. 2013. *Teaching the Critical Vocabulary of the Common Core.* Alexandria, VA: ASCD.

U.S. Department of Education, Office of English Language Acquisition. 2010. "Enhancement and Academic Achievement for Limited English Proficient Students." Accessed November 1, 2013, www.ncela.gwu.edu/files/uploads/9/growing_EL_0910.pdf.

Van Allen, Roach. 1964. "The Language Experience Approach" in *Teaching Young Children to Read,* edited by W.G. Gutts. Washington, DC: U.S. Office of Education.

Vygotsky, Lev S. 1978. *Mind in Society: The Development of Higher Psychological Processes.* Cambridge, MA: Harvard University Press.

Wang, Min, In Yeong Ko, and Jaeho Choi. 2009. "The Importance of Morphological Awareness in Korean-English Biliteracy Acquisition." *Contemporary Educational Psychology* 34: 132–142.

Wasik, Barbara, and Charlene Iannone-Campbell. 2012. "Developing Vocabulary Through Purposeful Strategic Conversations." *Reading Teacher* 66 (2): 321–332.

West, Michael. 1953. General Service List. Accessed September 25, 2013, http://www.academia.edu/4791005/Gsl-the-general-service-list-by-michael-west-195.

Wiggins, Grant, and Jay McTighe. 2005. *Understanding by Design, 2nd Edition.* Alexandria, VA: Association for Curriculum and Instruction.

Yopp, Hallie, Ruth Yopp, and Ashley Bishop. 2009. *Vocabulary Instruction for Academic Success.* Huntington Beach, CA: Shell Education.

Zarrillo, James J. 2011. *Ready for Revised RICA: A Test Preparation Guide for California's Reading Instruction Competence Assessment*, 3rd ed. Boston: Allyn & Bacon.

Zhang, Jie, Richard C. Anderson, Hong Li, Qiong Dong, Xinchun Wu, and Yan Zhang. 2010. "Cross-Language Transfer of Insight into the Structure of Compound Words." *Reading and Writing* 23: 311–336.

Zuñiga-Hill, Carmen, and Ruth Yopp. 1996. "Practices of Exemplary School Teachers of Second Language Learners." *Teacher Education Quarterly* 23 (1): 83–97.

Zuñiga Dunlap, Carmen and Evelyn Marino Weismann. 2006. *Helping English Language Learners Succeed*, 1st ed. Huntington Beach, CA: Shell Education.

Zwiers, Jeff, and Marie Crawford. 2009. "How to Start Academic Conversations." *Educational Leadership* 66 (7): 70–73.

Recommended Literature

Alborough, Jez. 2001. *Hug*. Somerville, MA: Candlewick Press.

Bishop, Nic. 2007. *Spiders*, 1st ed. New York: Scholastic Nonfiction.

Briggs, Raymond. 1978. *The Snowman*. New York: Random House.

Cole, Joanna. 1995. *Spider's Lunch: All About Garden Spiders*. New York: Grosset & Dunlap.

Day, Alexandra. 1985. *Good Dog, Carl*. New York: Farrar, Straus and Giroux.

dePaola, Tomie. 1978. *Pancakes for Breakfast*. Boston: HMH Books for Young Readers.

Gibbons, Gail. 1993. *Spiders*. New York: Holiday House.

Hürlmann, Ruth. 1980. *A velha árvore (The Old Tree)*. Sao Paulo, Brazil: Melhoramentos.

Kellogg, Steven. 1985. *Chicken Little*. New York: HarperCollins.

Lee, Suzy. 2008. *Wave*. San Francisco: Chronicle Books.

Lindgren, Astrid. 1950. *Pippi Longstocking*. New York: Viking Press.

Marsh, Laura. 2012. *National Geographic Readers: Spiders*. Des Moines, IA: National Geographic Children's Books.

Mayer, Mercer. 1999. *A Boy, a Dog, and a Frog*. St. Louis, MO: Turtleback Books.

Pinkney, Jerry. 2009. *The Lion and the Mouse*. New York: Little, Brown Company.

Pollard, Simon. 2004. *Hidden Spiders*. Boston: Rigby.

Series Books for Children

Benton, Jim. 2004–2013. *Dear Dumb Diary*. 15 vols. New York: Scholastic.

Bridwell, Norman. 1963–2013. *Clifford the Big Red Dog*. 100+ vols. New York: Scholastic.

Brown, Marc. 1976–2014. *Arthur*. 50+ vols. New York: Little Brown Books for Young Readers.

Kinney, Jeff. 2007–2013. *Diary of a Wimpy Kid*. 8 vols. New York: Harry N. Abrams.

Krulik, Nancy E. 2007–2010. *How I Survived Middle School*. 13 vols. New York: Scholastic.

Patterson, James. 2011–2014. *Middle School*. 6 vols. New York: Little Brown Books for Young Readers.

Peirce, Lincoln. *Big Nate*. 2010–2014. 13 vols. New York: HarperCollins.

Pilkey, Dav. 1997–2014. *Captain Underpants*. 12 vols. New York: The Blue Sky Press/Scholastic.

Rey, H. A., and Margaret Rey. *Curious George*. 45+ vols. New York: HMH Books for Young Readers.

Russell, Rachel Renée. 2009–2013. *Dork Diaries*. 10 vols. New York: Aladdin.

Answer Key

Anticipatory Quiz Answers

Chapter 1

1. False

2. True

3. False

4. True

5. False

6. False

Chapter 2

1. False

2. True

3. True

4. False

5. True

Chapter 3

1. False

2. True

3. False

4. True

5. False

Chapter 4

1. False

2. True

3. False

4. True

5. False

Chapter 5

1. False

2. False

3. False

4. False

5. False

6. False

7. True

Chapter 6

1. False

2. False

3. True

4. False

5. False

6. True

Chapter 7

1. False

2. True

3. True

4. False

5. True

6. True

Chapter 8

1. True

2. True

3. False

4. False

5. False

Application Activity: Selecting Key Vocabulary

Here is the suggested word selection from the passage on fossils:

1. *remains*   a. is typically not heard in everyday, conversational, nonacademic settings

2. *evidence*   f. appears frequently in texts across the curriculum

The remaining words are selected for the same rationales: d. promotes ongoing classroom instruction (within this unit of study), and g. builds rich connections to other words and concepts (also within this unit of study).

3. *sediment*

4. *silt*

5. *decay*

6. *bury*

Application Activity: Making Decisions About Concrete-to-Abstract Instruction

A discussion of each instructional unit below adds explanations and suggestions for literature studies.

Weather and climate: Scientists record data to compare patterns and make predictions

A literature study of *Sarah, Plain and Tall*

The ancient Roman Empire: Causes and effects of the expansion and disintegration of the Roman Empire

concrete   abstract

[◄───►]

Weather and Climate   *Sarah, Plain and Tall*
                                                                    Ancient Roman Empire

The Roman Empire

1. Weather and climate

Disciplinary Core Ideas: Scientists record patterns of weather across different times and areas so they can make predictions about what kind of weather might happen next (3–ESS2 Earth's Systems, NGSS 2013).

This science unit is placed close to the concrete end of the continuum because the important concepts can be unpacked and made visible in many ways. Students can be shown how to make and use bar graphs and pictographs to display data. Students and teachers can talk about graphs and what kind of data they show. Examining photos and video clips of natural disasters and their remedies can demonstrate how humans can reduce the impact of natural hazards. These are just two examples explaining how students can understand the key concepts in such a unit of study.

2. *Sarah, Plain and Tall* by Patricia MacLachlan

This beautiful story is difficult to unpack for English learners. It belongs at the extreme right of the continuum. First, the mid–American rural setting at the turn of the twentieth century is one that children today do not have experience with, unless through movies and television. Vocabulary from that era as well as from the descriptions of the natural world are plentiful, requiring intense "showing, not telling" to make meaning visible. However, the themes of family, coping, loss, and love are universal and should be explored through literature. It is more effective with English learners to read a book that addresses the same theme but in simpler language. Three examples of children's literature that also address family, loss, and coping are as follows:

- *Everett Anderson's Goodbye* by Lucille Clifton
- *Grandpa's Garden* by Shea Darian
- *The Tenth Good Thing About Barney* by Judith Viorst

3. The Roman Empire

"Analyze causes and effects of the vast expansion and ultimate disintegration of the Roman Empire." This area of study belongs at the abstract end of the continuum. The concepts in the social sciences are expressed almost exclusively through language, just as in the unit of study about ancient Egypt. Making abstract concepts comprehensible takes effort from both the teacher and students. Chapter 8 shows how a teacher plans a thematic unit on ancient Egypt. It includes many strategies that the teacher uses to make meaning tangible for English learners while also providing engaging learning activities for English-only students.

Teacher Resources

This appendix has several useful resources including two word lists that can be helpful when selecting vocabulary words for students to learn: the Common Core State Standards (CCSS) Critical Verbs and Nouns List and the Academic Word List (AWL).

Marilee Sprenger established the CCSS Critical Verbs and Nouns by selecting 29 verbs and 21 nouns of "words that are contained within the anchor standards and grade-level standards, and…that are used in the exemplars that are provided by the Common Core authors" (Sprenger 2013, 23). This appendix includes the critical verbs and nouns lists.

The AWL, created by Averil Coxhead, is made up of a total of 570 "head words" grouped into nine sublists (Coxhead 2000). This word list consists of those appearing most frequently in a corpus of 3.5 million words of running text in university textbooks in the arts, commerce, law, and science. This resource shows the first five sublists, in descending order from most frequently appearing to less frequently appearing.

By cross-referencing the words on the Critical Verbs and Nouns List and the AWL, terms common to both can be identified. Surprisingly, many CCSS words are not found on the AWL. Nor do many of the terms on the CCSS Critical Verbs and Nouns List appear on the General Service List (GSL), the 2,284 most commonly appearing words in the English language. That is, they are unique to the CCSS Critical Verbs and Nouns List, and they are identified in bold text in the chart. Given the words' lack of appearance in other sources and the importance of the CCSS words, teachers should take special care to provide instruction on these words. As a way to further sift relevant and academically important vocabulary words, teachers should become familiar with and teach the CCSS verbs and nouns most commonly used for their particular grade level.

CCSS Critical Verbs and Nouns List

29 Critical Verbs	21 Critical Nouns
1. **analyze**	1. alliteration
2. **articulate**	2. analogy
3. **cite**	3. argument
4. compare (GSL)	4. central idea
5. **comprehend**	5. **conclusions**
6. **contrast**	6. **connections**
7. **delineate**	7. **connotative language**
8. **demonstrate**	8. details (GSL)
9. describe (GSL)	9. **evidence**
10. determine (GSL)	10. **figurative language**
11. develop (GSL)	11. **illustrations**
12. distinguish (GSL)	12. **interaction**
13. draw (GSL)	13. **metaphor**
14. **evaluate**	14. **mood**
15. explain (GSL)	15. **point of view**
16. **identify**	16. rhetoric
17. **infer**	17. simile
18. **integrate**	18. stanza
19. interpret	19. structure
20. **locate**	20. theme
21. organize (GSL)	21. tone
22. **paraphrase**	
23. refer (GSL)	
24. **retell**	
25. suggest (GSL)	
26. summarize (GSL *summary*)	
27. support (GSL)	
28. **synthesize**	
29. **trace**	

Adapted from Sprenger 2013

Academic Word List

This resource shows the first five sublists of the AWL. The bold words are those that also appear on Sprenger's CCSS list.

Sublist 1

analyze	contract	export	legal	respond
approach	create	factor	legislature	role
area	data	finance	major	section
assess	define	formula	method	sector
assume	derive	function	occur	significant
authority	distribute	**identify**	percent	similar
available	economy	income	period	source
benefit	environment	indicate	policy	specific
concept	establish	individual	principle	**structure**
consist	estimate	interpret	proceed	theory
constitute	evident	involve	process	
context	**evidence**	issue	require	
		labor	research	

Sublist 2

achieve	compute	**evaluate**	obtain	secure
acquire	conclude	feature	participate	seek
administer	conduct	final	perceive	select
affect	consequent	focus	primary	site
appropriate	construct	impact	purchase	strategy
aspect	consume	injure	range	survey
assist	credit	institute	region	text
category	culture	invest	regulate	tradition
chapter	design	item	relevant	transfer
commission	distinct	journal	reside	
community	element	maintain	resource	
complex	equate	normal	restrict	

Academic Word List *(cont.)*

Sublist 3

alternative	corporate	illustrate	minor	scheme
circumstance	correspond	**illustrations**	negate	sequence
comment	criteria	immigrate	outcome	sex
compensate	deduce	imply	partner	shift
component	**demonstrate**	initial	philosophy	specify
consent	document	instance	physical	sufficient
considerable	dominate	interact	proportion	task
constant	emphasis	justify	publish	technical
constrain	ensure	layer	react	technique
contribute	exclude	link	register	technology
convene	framework	**locate**	rely	valid
coordinate	fund	maximum	remove	volume
core				

Sublist 4

access	confer	hence	occupy	promote
adequate	**contrast**	hypothesis	option	regime
annual	cycle	implement	output	resolve
apparent	debate	implicate	overall	retain
approximate	despite	impose	parallel	series
attitude	dimension	**integrate**	parameter	statistic
attribute	domestic	internal	phase	status
civil	emerge	investigate	predict	stress
code	error	job	principal	subsequent
commit	ethnic	label	prior	sum
communicate	goal	mechanism	professional	summary
concentrate	grant	obvious	project	undertake

Academic Word List *(cont.)*

Sublist 5				
academy	decline	facilitate	monitor	revenue
adjust	discrete	fundamental	network	stable
alter	draft	generate	notion	style
amend	enable	generation	objective	substitute
aware	energy	image	orient	sustain
capacity	enforce	liberal	perspective	symbol
challenge	entity	license	precise	target
clause	equivalent	logic	prime	transit
compound	evolve	margin	psychology	trend
conflict	expand	medical	pursue	version
consult	expose	mental	ratio	welfare
contact	external	modify	reject	whereas

Adapted from Coxhead 2000

Retelling Rubric

Student: _____

Text: _____

Check one:

	Text was read aloud to student.
	Text was read aloud by student.
	Text was read silently by student.
	Text was read aloud with student partner.

Other notes or information:

Printed with permission from Zuñiga Dunlap and Marino Weismann 2006

Retelling Rubric *(cont.)*

Text recall of . . .	0	1	2	3	4
Sequence					
Main idea(s)					
Supporting ideas					
Important information					
Language Use					
Vocabulary					
Sentence structure (grammar)					
Capitalization and punctuation					
Spelling					
Text Response or Reaction					
Personal observations					
Creative impressions					
Text extension					
Connections across text					

Scoring:

0	No evidence
1	Limited evidence
2	Moderate evidence
3	Substantial evidence
4	Excellent

Holistic Writing Rubric for English Language Learners

	1	2	3	4	5	6
Content and Ideas ___/6	Great difficulty expressing any content or idea; no support provided	Scant conveyance of content or idea; may provide limited support	Presents content or idea; may stay on topic but content is meager; may provide some but incomplete support for ideas	Topic development is evident; evidence of weak to adequate support for ideas	Sufficient content and ideas and support for these is provided; could use stronger or additional development	Clearly conveys ideas and provides strong support
Organization ___/6	No logical organization pattern; very difficult to understand	Attempts to express and organize ideas but difficult to understand; no paragraph structure or transitions across ideas	Some key ideas are evident, although the piece meanders; some evidence of paragraph formation; a lack in the overall organization	Ideas are organized; clear evidence of paragraph structure; may lack opening and closing statements; may lack completely clear or smooth flow of ideas.	Ideas are clearly organized; clear evidence of paragraph structure; may lack opening and closing statements; may lack completely clear or smooth flow of ideas.	Well organized; clear use of paragraphs; opening and closing statements; writing is clear and well-ordered
Word Choice ___/6	Rudimentary vocabulary; very basic stage of vocabulary development	Limited vocabulary; difficulty expressing basic ideas	Vocabulary is sufficient to express basic ideas in a simplistic manner	Vocabulary is sufficient to convey ideas with limited to some variety in word choice	Adequate word choices; good variety in vocabulary	Vocabulary demonstrates a level comparable to fluent English speakers

Holistic Writing Rubric for English Language Learners *(cont.)*

	1	2	3	4	5	6
Details ___/6	No details or description, evident	Weak details limited to phrases or fragments found inconsistenly	Some details are evident and may provide thin description	Adequate details and description are generally used throughout the piece	Adequate to substantial details and description to support main ideas	Conveys details clearly and consistently; comparable to fluent English speakers.
Conventions ___/6	Grammar and conventions are rudimentary or lacking; writing consists of single words, sentence fragments or phrases; poor spelling	Poor grammar and conventions make writing difficult to understand; some words are spelled correctly but many are not	Modest control of grammar and conventions; contains mis-spellings, ungrammatical structures, choppy or run-on sentences and/or no sentence variety, but the piece is comprehensible	Adequate grammar and conventions, although not perfect; use of some sentence variety; writing is understandable; adequate spelling	Good control of grammar and conventions; evidence of varied sentence structures; spelling approaches that of fluent English speaker	Nearly perfect use of grammar and conventions; good sentence variety and clear, well-formed paragraphs, correct spelling
Total Score: ___/30						

Printed with permission from Zuñiga Dunlap and Marino Weismann 2006

Thematic Unit Organizational Framework

Key Concepts
Key Grammatical Structures (fluent English and advanced EL)
Key Grammatical Structures (beginning and intermediate EL)

Thematic Unit Organizational Framework *(cont.)*

Relevant Common Core State Standards			
Assessment (fluent English)		**Assessment (English learners)**	
Domain-Specific Vocabulary	Derivations of Domain-Specific Vocabulary	ELD Vocabulary	Procedural Verbs

Oral Assessment Activity

Notes

Notes

Notes

Notes